I0023027

George Drake, James Fuller Brown

History of the First Baptist Church of Piscataway : with an account of its bi-centennial celebration, June 20th, 1889, and sketches of pioneer progenitors of Piscataway planters

George Drake, James Fuller Brown

History of the First Baptist Church of Piscataway : with an account of its bi-centennial celebration, June 20th, 1889, and sketches of pioneer progenitors of Piscataway planters

ISBN/EAN: 9783337261054

Printed in Europe, USA, Canada, Australia, Japan

Cover: Foto ©Lupo / pixelio.de

More available books at **www.hansebooks.com**

HISTORY

OF THE

FIRST BAPTIST CHURCH OF PISCATAWAY

WITH AN ACCOUNT OF ITS

BI-CENTENNIAL CELEBRATION

JUNE 20th, 1889,

AND SKETCHES OF

PIONEER PROGENITORS OF PISCATAWAY PLANTERS.

STELTON, N. J,

1889.

GEO. DRAKE,
P. A. RUNYON, } Committee
W. H. STELLE, } on Publication.

NEW YORK:
PAKENHAM & DOWLING,
STEAM PRINTERS,
12 and 14 Spruce Street.

1889.

CONTENTS.

At a regular Church Meeting held May 26, 1889, the following resolutions were passed:

"*Resolved,* That this Church deem it in every way fitting and due that we hold suitable memorial services at our approaching Bi-Centennial, and that a committee be appointed to prepare and submit to the Church a program for the celebration, including time, subjects, speakers and other arrangements for the occasion.

"*Resolved,* That such committee consist of the Pastor, Rev. J. W. Sarles, and brethren P. R. Letson, and P. A. Runyon."

After full consultation the committee appointed Thursday, June 20th, 1889, as the day for the Anniversary, arranged a Program for the celebration, and sent the invitation appearing below to all the Baptist Churches in New Jersey and such churches and individuals elsewhere, as were for special reasons, interested in the occasion.

——GREETING.——

DEAR BRETHREN AND SISTERS:

The Piscataway Baptist Church will (D. V.) hold its Bi-Centennial on Thursday, June 20th, 1889.

On an occasion of so much gratitude to us, and of such common interest to the whole Baptist family of New Jersey, we shall be happy to see the faces of so many of you, and your associates in the Sanctuary, as can spend the day with us.

Exercises are to begin promptly at 10.30 A.M., and continue through the day and evening.

REV. J. W. SARLES, ⎫ *Bi-Centenary*
P. A. RUNYON, ⎬ *Committee.*
P. R. LETSON, ⎭

BI-CENTENNIAL PROGRAM.

—: FORENOON, 10.30 O'CLOCK.:—

1. *Organ.* - - - - - Miss Maria C. Sarles.
2. *Doxology.*
3. *Invocation,* - - - - By the Pastor.
4. *Anthem,* - - - - By the Choir.
5. *Scripture,* Ps., 48:1—14. - Rev. M. MacGregor, New York.
6. *Prayer,* - - - - Rev. C. J. Page.
7. *Hymn, No. 271,* - - "All hail the power of Jesus' name."
8. *Greeting,* - - - - By the Pastor.
9. *History of the Church* (Part 1st), - - - - -
   by J. F. Brown, D.D., Pastor from 1868-78.
10. *Hymn, No. 748,* - - "Zion stands with hills surrounded,—"
11. *Middletown Baptist Church.* 1688. Pastor Rev. E. E. Jones.
12. *Cohansey Baptist Church,* 1690, Pastor Harry Tratt (not present)
13. *Hymn, No. 637.* - - - "I love thy kingdom, Lord."
14. *Scotch Plains Baptist Church,* 1747. Pastor J. H. Parks, D.D.
15. *Prayer,* - - Rev. Mr. Livermore, of New Market, N. J.
16. *Hymn No. 416,* - - - "Rock of ages, cleft for me."
17. *Benediction,* - - Rev. R. T. Middleditch, D.D , New York.

COLLATION.

—: AFTERNOON, 2.30 O'CLOCK. :—

1. *Anthem.*

2. *Invocation,* - - Rev. Geo. H. Gardner, South River, N. J.

3. *Scripture.* Ps., 67: 1-7. 20. 1-9, Rev. G. F. Love, Princeton, N. J.

4. *Prayer,* - - - - Rev. Mr. Young, Allentown, N. J.

5. *Hymn, No. 553,* - "Oh, could we speak the matchless worth."

6. *History of the Church* (concluded), - - Dr. J. F. Brown.

7. *Note* from Mrs. C. L. Lee and Mrs. C. P. Farson, surviving daughters of the 7th Pastor, Rev. Daniel Lewis.

8. *Bi-Centennial Hymn,* - - Abraham Coles, L.L.D.

9. *Geneological Sketches,* - - - O. B. Leonard, Esq.

10. *Letter* - - - from Ezra M. Hunt, M.D., Trenton, N. J.

11. *Morristown Baptist Church,* 1752, Pastor Rev. Addison Parker.

12. *Hymn, No. 413,* - - - - "Jesus! lover of my soul."

13. *Philadelphia Baptist Association,* 1707-1791,
Moderator J. W. Willmarth, D.D.

14. *Philadelphia Baptist Association,*
President of the Board, Hon. Horatio Gates Jones.

15. *New Brooklyn Baptist Church,* 1792, Pastor Rev. A. Armstrong.

16. *Hymn, No. 982,* - - - "Jerusalem, my happy home."

17. *First Baptist Church, New Brunswick,* 1816,
Pastor Rev. H. C. Applegarth, Jr.

18. *Wm. H. Parmly, D. D.,* President of the N. J. Education Society.

19. *Rev. W. V. Wilson,* Helper of all Good Institutions, (not present.)

20. *Hymn, No. 213,* - "What are those soul-reviving strains."

21. *Benediction,* - - - Rev. G. E. Horr, Summit, N. J.

SUPPER.

—: EVENING, 7.30 O'CLOCK. :—

1. *Service of Song.*

2. *Scripture.* Jno. 15:1-16,   Rev. R. T. Middleditch, D.D., New York.

3. *Prayer,* -   -   -   - Rev. F. R. Morse, D. D., New York.

4. *Hymn, No. 280,* -   -   " Come, let us join our cheerful songs.'

5. *First Baptist Church, Plainfield,* 1818, Pastor D. J. Yerkes, D.D.

6. *New Market Baptist Church,* 1852, Pastor Rev. J. A. Cubberley.

7. *Warren Randolph, D. D.,* of Newport, R. I., Licentiate.   Letter.

8. *Hymn No. 968,* -   -   -   " Who are these in bright array."

9. *Rev. C. J. Page,*   Pastor of this Church from 1857 to 1867.

10. *Remsen Avenue Baptist Church, New Brunswick,*
    Rev. M. V. McDuffie.

11. *Hymn, No. 743.* -   -   " Happy the church, thou sacred place."

12. *Rev. C. C. Smith,* of Hempstead, L. I., Licentiate.   Poem.

13. *Rev. Wm. Rollinson,* of Rahway, N. J., one of the Senior Pastors.

14. *Prayer.*

15. *Closing Words.*

16. *Hymn, No. 985,* -   -   " Beyond the smiling and the weeping,"

17. *Benediction,* -   -   -   -   - Rev. M. V. McDuffie.

It was regretted by all, that three of the Brethren were prevented, for want of time on the day of the Celebration, from responding for their churches or societies. Two of them, at the solicitation of the Publication Committee furnished the substance of their intended remarks and they appear in this volume. The remaining brother, Dr. Parmly, was absent from home when the request was made, which probably prevented him from complying with it.

RESOLUTIONS OF THANKS ADOPTED BY THE CHURCH.

"WHEREAS, Our former beloved Pastor, Rev. J. F. Brown, D. D., very kindly acceded to our request to prepare for our Bi-Centenary a history of this church ; and

"WHEREAS, He has withheld neither time nor labor to make it exhaustive and complete, and has thereby secured for us and for our children a rich legacy bequeathed to us by the fathers and mothers in this Church who have gone before us; therefore

"RESOLVED, That we tender him our united thanks, assuring him that we keenly appreciate this generous and unrequited contribution to our spiritual advantage.

"RESOLVED, That we also extend our thanks to O. B. Leonard, Esq, of Plainfield, N. J., for his interesting paper on the "Pioneer Progenitors of Piscataway Planters.

"RESOLVED, That our warm thanks are due and are hereby tendered to the organist and choir from Brooklyn, for the inspiring music that did so much to move our hearts and enhance the enjoyment of all the other services of our Bi-Centennial.

"RESOLVED, That we thank Mr. James Rogers, of New Brunswick, for doing so much to add to the comfort of our guests at table.

"RESOLVED, That we tender to Mr. White, representative of the Mutual Life Insurance Company of New York, our united thanks for the use of the house located at Stelton, for the accommodation of our guests June 20, 1889, at the celebration of the Bi-Centennial Anniversary of our Church.

"MOVED, That a copy of the foregoing Resolutions be sent to each of the parties named and that they be entered upon the minutes of the Church."

A HISTORY

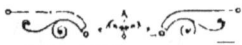

PREFATORY NOTE.

The writer of the following historical sketch is greatly indebted for valuable information to O. B. Leonard, Esq., of Plainfield, who has made the study of Colonial times and the genealogy of the early settlers a specialty ; also, to Miss Henrietta Dayton, of Stelton, for the loan of old minutes of Associations which have been handed down by her ancestors for nearly a hundred years; also, to Mr. Samuel E. Stelle, Mr. Peter A. Runyon, Mr. Peter R. Letson and Miss Laura J. Runyon for statistical accounts, investigations of a various nature, family genealogies, etc., and especially to " Whitehead's History of New Jersey under the Proprietors," a work of inestimable value to the student of Colonial times.　　　　　　　　　　J. F. B.

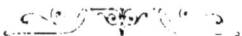

HISTORY OF THE

FIRST BAPTIST CHURCH,

OF PISCATAWAY, N. J.

BY J. F. BROWN, D. D.

Two centuries have elapsed since this Church was constituted an independent Church of baptised believers in Christ Jesus. Since then, generation after generation has passed away, but the Church still lives, and, to-day, with a spiritual force not only unabated but the rather greatly augmented, stands on the threshold of the third century, strong in faith, and bright with the hope that He, who was with their fathers, will also be with them in the power of his Spirit, and with their children and children's children, and work out through them his purposes of grace and glory.

It is eminently fit and proper that this Church, in view of the completion of its bi-centennial life, should commemorate the fact in general assembly with representatives of sister churches, and abundantly utter the memory of the Lord's great goodness, and unite in thanksgiving and praise for the grace that has been so signally displayed throughout its history. "Let Israel rejoice in Him that made him." "One generation shall praise Thy works to another, and shall declare Thy mighty acts."

To me has been assigned by the Church the onerous but not unwelcome task of gathering and arranging the materials of its history, and thus tracing it connectedly from its organization to the present time. It is a deplorable fact that no records or minutes of the Church exist prior to the month of August, 1781. They were destroyed during the Revolutionary war, either by marauding bands of British soldiers when their army was in possession of New Brunswick,[1] or—which is more probable—they were carried off or destroyed by the Clerk of the Church at that time who, according to tradition, was a Tory. From whence, then, are our sources of history?—From Colonial documents, township records, the researches of Morgan Edwards and Dr. Benedict, the Century Minutes of the Philadelphia Association and fragmentary papers on early Baptist history. From such sources we learn that this Church was constituted in the year 1689, the very year following that of the great revolution in England which secured the overthrow of the last of the Stuart Dynasty, and led to the elevation of William and Mary to the throne.

But whence came the constituent members; and when, and why? To answer these questions intelligently we must have recourse to Colonial history. New Jersey was at this time under what was known as the "Proprietory" form of government. In the year 1664, Charles II, King of England, made a gift of territory lying between the western side of Connecticut River and the east side of Delaware Bay to his brother, James, the Duke of York, afterwards King of England under the title of James II. The Duke, not caring to take the personal supervision of this territory, transferred so much of it as is now New Jersey to Lord John Berkley, Baron of Stratton, and Sir George Carteret, of Saltrum, in Devon. The Dutch, who had been in possession of a considerable portion of this territory and had formed many settlements and exercised governmental rights, yielded to the superior power of Britain, and by the treaty of Breda, in 1667, the possession of New Amsterdam (New York) and of New Jersey was confirmed to the English.[2]

Lord Berkley and Sir George Carteret having thus become sole proprietors of New Jersey, were disposed, with a view, doubtless, to the rapid peopling of the territory, to grant very liberal terms to new settlers. On the 10th of February, 1664, O. S., they signed a constitution which they issued to people far and near, under the title of "The Concessions and Agreements of the Lord Proprietors of New Jersey to and with all and every of the Adventurers and all such as shall Settle and Plant there." One item of these Concessions was as follows: "That no person qualified as aforesaid within the said

---

1. The same is true of the records of the First Presbyterian Church, of Newark. "It is much to be regretted that the records of the Church, extending from the year 1666 to the time of the Revolutionary war, were destroyed when the British troops had possession of the town in 1776, and those which remain date back only to 1781."—*Dr. Stearns' Historical Discourses.*

2. Whitehead's New Jersey under the Proprietors, p. 27.

Province at any time shall be anyways molested, punished, disquieted, or called in question for any difference in opinion or practice in matters of religious concernment, who do not actually disturb the civil peace of the said Province, but that all and every such person and persons may, from time to time, and at all times, freely and fully have and enjoy his and their judgments and consciences in matters of religion throughout the said Province."[1] This document has the ring of liberty, civil and religious. The rights of conscience are here recognized—the boon hitherto denied in all the settlements on the Continent, save in that of the Providence plantations, in Rhode Island, where Roger Williams, thirty years before, had founded a government on "the sanctity of conscience, or soul-freedom."[2]

On the same day that these Concessions were published, Berkley and Carteret appointed Philip Carteret, a relative of Sir George, the Governor of the Province, instructing him to carry out the provisions of the Concessions. He, in obedience to this instruction, immediately sent messengers into New England to make known the liberal character of the government of New Jersey. The effect of these Concessions on the minds of all in New England who had suffered from the intolerance of the Puritans, can better be imagined than described. Henceforth the fertile plains of New Jersey, together with its salubrious climate, loomed up before them as a land of promise. Indeed, it is recorded by an old writer of that period that it was thought by some "worthy the name of Paradise," because, in addition to its natural advantages, "it had no lawyers, or physicians, or parsons"[3]—a keen thrust, evidently, at Puritan parsons and those of the Church of England. It will occasion no surprise that people living in New England came into these parts in large numbers, singly and by families, or colonies, and formed settlements, generally as close to the sea as possible, and along the bays, sounds and rivers, stretching from Newark to Middletown and Shrewsbury. They came not all in one year, but at different dates extending from the time of a few original associates in 1666 and 1668 to the time of the transfer of the government from the Proprietors to the Crown in 1702. Nor did they all come from New England, but from the mother country and Scotland, and from New York, particularly from Long Island; all influenced by a desire to advance their temporal comfort, many by a yet stronger

1. Volume Grants and Concessions.
2. Bancroft's History of the United States.
3. Whitehead's East New Jersey under the Proprietors.

desire to escape from civil and religious tyranny and enjoy freedom to worship God without molestation by civil magistrates. This statement, with regard to the settlers of Newark in 1666, is to be received with some qualification. They came from Connecticut and were Congregationalists or of the Standing Order, who, having become disaffected towards the General Court of Connecticut because of the Half-way Covenant, formed a colony and emigrated to Newark with the design of there founding a government that should be ruled and conducted only by members of the Congregational Church. No others were to be " admitted as Freemen or Free Burgesses within our town upon Passaic River." No others were to be chosen to magistracy or to carry on any kind of civil judicature or as deputies or assistants, to have power to vote in establishing laws, and making and repealing them ; nor shall any but such church members have any vote in any such elections."[1] Here was a repetition of Puritan folly, the first and last attempt to combine Church and State in the province of New Jersey, and which, happily, in the course of a generation, yielded to the more enlightened and liberal principles which then prevailed and had been embodied in the Concessions of the Lord Proprietors. Very different in opinion and purpose were the settlers in the districts of Middletown and Piscataway, some of whom had, in New England, suffered for conscience sake under the rule of the Puritans. The most of those at Middletown were Baptists. Some were Quakers, mostly from Long Island, who had endured oppression there under the Dutch administration. All these sought freedom, not for themselves alone, but for all who bore the image of God.

Middletown received its charter in 1665 ; Piscataway, December 18, 1666. The names of those to whom was made the first conveyance of lands by Deputy Surveyor under Carteret, were John Martin, Charles Gillman, Hugh Dunn and Hopewell Hull. They and their associates founded the town of Piscataway.[2] In 1685 this township with its outlying plantations was supposed to contain forty thousand acres of land, inhabited by eighty families or about four hundred people. This township was reduced in size in the year 1798, and in 1870 was still farther reduced by the formation of another township out of it, called Raritan, in which township this house of worship is now situated.

The names of those who came into the township after its formation in 1665, were those of Dennis, Smith, Drake and Dunham in 1668 ;

1. Newark Town Records.
2. Whitehead's East Jersey under the Proprietors.

of Fitz-Randolph, Langstaff and Hendrick, in 1669; of Sutton, Manning, Smalley, Bonham, 1670-'75 ; of Runyon and Wooding, in 1683 ; of Giles, Dayton, Bishop, Mullinson, Munday, Higgins, Laing, Coriell, Webster, 1680-1685 ; of Blackford, Pyatt and Field, in 1695 ; of Stelle and Clarkson, from New York, in 1705. Some of the earliest settlers came first from New Hampshire, on the left side of the Piscataqua River, but at a later date from Long Island. These were mostly Baptists. New Hampshire was at that time under the jurisdiction of the Massachusetts Bay Company, and, of course, was not exempt from Puritan interference. Nevertheless, some of the sect everywhere spoken against, living near Dover, were wont to assemble at that point for divine worship. How long they had been settled in that region, history does not inform us. But they were there in the year 1638, for in the same year they were ministered to by the celebrated Hanserd Knollys. This gentleman graduated at the University of Cambridge, and in 1629 was ordained as a minister of the established Church by the Bishop of Peterboro. His labors, in connection with that Church, were abundant. In a short time he became convinced from study of the Scriptures, that he could no longer consistently remain in connection with the establishment. Subjected to persecution on account of his dissent, he took passage in an emmigrant vessel bound for Boston. On his arrival there the Puritan Ministers, ever on the scent for opinions differing from their own, reported him to the Magistrates as an Anabaptist, and, strangely enough and untruthfully, as an Antinomian, therefore a dangerous man and "unfit to remain in that patent." A stranger in a strange land and penniless, he was compelled to resort to daily labor in order to get bread for himself and wife. Providentially he soon fell in with one or two men who had come from Dover to Boston on business. By them he was invited to go with them to Dover. He accepted their invitation and there ministered to a congregation composed mostly of a few Baptist families. He remained till the close of the year 1641 and then, at the urgent request of his aged father, returned to England.[1] Our limited space forbids a detailed account of the petty annoyances and trials to which these Dover Baptists were subjected by the oppressive Church and State jurisdiction of Massachusetts.

1. After Mr. Knollys returned to England, he was ordained pastor of a Baptist Church in Great St. Helen street, London, in the year 1645, and continued in that relation till his death in 1691, in the 93d year of his age. He was contemporary with Keach and Kiffin, and Bunyan, and held in universal esteem by all good men as a devout Christian, an accomplished scholar, and a laborious pastor. While in New England, Cotton Mather, in his Magnalia, refers to him as "a godly Anabaptist, and having a respectable character in the churches of this wilderness."

Soon after the departure of Mr. Knollys, they too, seeing no hope of deliverance from their trials in New England, emigrated to Long Island, then under the Dutch government, where they remained until New York came under the power of the English in 1664. There new trials befel them. Harrassed either by officials of the Dutch government, or by the tyrannical measures of the Episcopal establishment that followed the Dutch rule, they sold out their property, and, gladly availing themselves of the larger liberty proffered by the Proprietors, they came in the year 1666 to this part of New Jersey and found a permanent home. They did not come *as a Church*, nor is there any evidence that they maintained any organization after they left New Hampshire ; and even there, it was as a society or band of baptised believers that they existed, not as a regularly constituted Baptist Church. They were largely men of social influence and standing. Some of them were, as already noticed, patentees of the township which they chose to call, after that of their old home in New Hampshire, Piscataway ; or, New Piscataway, this latter name being so written in the Town Book.[1]

How many of the settlers were Baptists, or became such after the original settlement, history does not state. More than one writer preceding and succeeding the formation of the Church, alludes to them as forming no inconsiderable part of the population. An Episcopal rector who preached at Amboy in 1711, writing to the Secretary of the "Society for the Propagation of the Gospel in Foreign Parts," informs him that "the Anabaptists swarmed in these parts," and that they held meetings in the Town House. This Town House stood in the village then, as now, known as "Piscatawaytown," a place of more political importance then than now, being through a long period of Colonial times the seat of justice for a large extent of territory extending over Middlesex and parts of what are now Union and Somerset Counties. The Colonial Legislature also held one session, if not more, in this place. New Brunswick then had no existence. The road

1. Whether Hanserd Knollys ever preached to any Baptists that formed the constituency of this Church, is a matter of grave doubt. Nearly fifty years elapsed after he returned to England before this Church was organized. If, therefore, they sat under his ministry in New Hampshire, they must have been very young people then, or now of advanced years—at least 68 or 70 years of age—but some of them lived many years ; John Drake, fifty years after the organization of the Church, or about one hundred years after the ministry of Hanserd Knollys at Dover. He, at least, could not have been a member of the Dover flock in Hanserd Knollys' time. The same must be true of Edmund Dunham, (who lived many years after 1689), and indeed of the other four constituents, none of whom can we suppose to have been men just tottering on the verge of the grave when this Church was formed. The more rational supposition, therefore, is, that some of the constituents were sons and daughters of the old Dover Baptists of Hanserd Knollys' time, and that they, after their sojourn on Long Island, came to this neighborhood, and, strong in the faith of their fathers, planted a Church of the same faith.

passing through this village was the only one that connected Amboy with the settlements of Middletown and Shrewsbury. Passengers were ferried over the Raritan at a point opposite a tract on which now lies New Brunswick, called " Mion's Ferry." As for other roads they were little more than bridle-paths through forests abounding with deer and game of almost every sort. The Indians, from whom all the lands of East Jersey were bought for what they, in their innocence, considered a fair equivalent, were peculiarly peaceful and gentle, so that we read of no depredations committed by them on the property of the settlers, much less of their taking up arms against them.

The Town House was built in 1685-6. This appears from an item in the Official Record at Trenton, liber 4, which reads *verbatim*, thus: "Jan. 18, 1685-6. At the Town Meetinge then agreed yt there should be a meetinge house built forthwith, the dimensions as followeth : Twenty foot wide, thirty foot longue and ten foot between joynts." This house, though not of magnificent proportions nor of ornate architecture, was deemed ample for the purpose for which it was designed. Let not the phraseology employed to describe this house beget the idea that it was designed exclusively or chiefly as a house of worship. It was built rather for municipal business, for holding courts, and for the consideration and discussion of matters appertaining to the public good. It was emphatically a Town Hall in the modern sense of this term. Yet its use for holding religious meetings was likewise contemplated, as might naturally be inferred from the religious character of the settlers, apart from any positive evidence that it was so used. A Town House in a community that "swarmed with Anabaptists" would scarcely be put up without reference to its being used for divine worship ; and we know it was so used. There your Baptist ancestors, the Drakes and Dunns and Martins and Suttons and Daytons and Runyons and Stelles met together and worshipped God in spirit and in truth. Nor is it difficult for us to imagine how profound must have been their gratitude that there were none to molest or make them afraid in their new asylum of liberty.

Between this unpretentious " Meetinge House " and the dwellings of the people there was, as we infer from the records of those times, a general correspondence. These also were of simple, and often rude structure, yet good enough to meet the reasonable demands of dwellers in a new country. Garvin Laurie, Deputy Governor of East Jersey, writing to a friend of his in London under date of East Jersey, March 26, 1684, after speaking of the variety of forest trees and of the abund-

ance of fish and oysters, of fowl and pork and venison, and the cheap-
ness of the products of the soil, says : " We have good brick earth
and stone for building at Amboy and elsewhere, the Countrie farm
houses are built very cheap; a Carpenter with a man's own servants
builds the house ; they have all materials for nothing, except Nails ;
their chimneys are of stones ; they make their own Ploughs and Carts
for the most part, only the Iron work is very dear. The poorer sort
set up a house of two or three rooms themselves after this manner :
The walls are of cloven timber, about 8 or 10 inches broad, like planks
set on end to the ground and the other nailed to the raising which they
plaister within ; they build a barn after the same manner and these not
above 5 *lib.* apiece ; and then to work they go ; 2 or 3 men in one year
will clear 50 acres, in some places 60, in others more." And in another
letter we are told that " the Coverings to their Houses are mostly
Shingles made of Oak, Chestnut and Cedar wood, which makes a very
neat covering, yet there are some houses covered after the Dutch
manner with pantikles."[1]   These extracts are here given in order to
convey to the present generation some idea of the manner in which
their worthy ancestors lived and toiled, of their habitations, in a word,
of their simple home-life. If their style of living was primitive, and
devoid of modern comfort and luxuriousness, we can, nevertheless,
easily conceive how happy and restful in mind they were, and how
willing to endure the toils and hardships incident to pioneer life when
they contrasted their peaceful condition with that of thousands in the
mother country and on the Continent, many of them of like faith,
against whom even now under the infamous reigns of Charles II. and
James II., the waves of persecution were fiercely beating.[2]

These years of tribulation abroad wrought no abridgement of the
civil and religious rights of the settlers in New Jersey. Amid all
political changes and the shiftings of administrations, they found what
here they sought, freedom to worship God, and were thankful. The
twenty-four Proprietors into whose hands the ownership of New Jersey
passed in 1682, among whom were William Penn and Robert Barclay,[3]
were men who respected the rights of conscience. It was during the
government by these Proprietors that the three oldest churches of our

1. Whitehead's East Jersey under the Proprietors, pp. 120, 121.
2. Nearly eight thousand Protestant Dissenters perished in prison in the days of
King Charles II., merely for dissenting from the Church of England, (in matters of faith
and Church government) and for no other cause were stifled, I had almost said, murdered,
in jails for their religion.—*Quoted from Defoe, by Trimey.*
3. Author of the "Apology for the Doctrines and Principles of the Quakers," and
for a short time Governor of the Province.

denomination came into existence; that at Middletown in 1688; this Church a few months afterwards, in 1689, and the Church at Cohansey in 1690. This Church was the twelfth if not the tenth one organized on this Continent.[1] We know not in what month of the year 1689 this Church was constituted, nor is it indispensable we should know, however gratifying it would be to our curiosity to know not only the month, but the day, and the time of day, and all the circumstances attending so memorable an event. Reliable records inform us that of the settlers up to 1689, (the names of some of whom have already been given), and the larger part of whom were doubtless Baptists in sentiment, only six men formed the constituency of the Church. Their names were:

HUGH DUNN,	JOHN DRAKE,
EDMUND DUNHAM,	NICHOLAS BONHAM,
JOHN SMALLEY,	JOHN RANDOLPH.

All these names, except one, are now on the Register of the Church, showing that all through the generations following, in the place of the fathers have come the children. Dr. Benedict, in his " History of the Baptists," fitly remarks that " were we to judge of the religious faith of these settlers by the lists of members in the two Baptist churches in Piscataway, we should infer they were of that Denomination, most of the names being found on those lists." This was written seventy-five years ago, and the same might be said now. The six brethren named above were constituted a Baptist Church some time in the Spring of 1689, according to Edwards, through the official ministrations of Rev. Thomas Killingsworth, the same brother who had performed a like service for the brethren at Middletown.[1]

It is strange that the name of no female appears among the constituent members of our three oldest churches in the State. These constituent members numbered thirty-two men. It is known that some, perhaps the most of them, were heads of families. That their wives generally were one with them in faith and in the hope of the Gospel, is not to be doubted. Utterly unable to account for the omission of

---

1. Dr. Benedict states (History of the Baptists, vol. 1, p. 503) that the Church of Tiverton " was the seventh Baptist Church formed on the American Continent." If so, Piscataway was the tenth.

2. Too much can scarcely be said in praise of the eminent labors of this servant of the Lord. A native of Norwich, Eng., and ordained in that country, he came to America and engaged earnestly in the work of the ministry. During one of his itinerating tours through the Province of New Jersey, he visited Middletown, where he seems to have been mainly instrumental in effecting the organization of that Church. It was probably during the same tour that he visited the Baptists in Piscataway and performed a like service for them. In the following year he officiated at the constitution of the Cohansey Church, in the neighborhood of which he had previously fixed his residence. He was called to the pastorate of the new Church and continued in that relation till his death in 1708. Mr. Killingsworth was also a Judge of the Salem Court. That he was an honored citizen and esteemed minister of Christ, the records of the times fully confirm.

the names of noble women among the constituent members, the fact only can be noted with unfeigned regret.

Of the foregoing six constituent members of this Church three were exhorters, or lay-preachers, namely: John Drake, Hugh Dunn and Edmund Dunham. Mr. Dunham afterwards became a Seventh-Day Baptist, and was one of the constituent members and the first pastor of the Sabbatarian Church near the settlement now known as New Market. The account of his conversion to Sabbatarian sentiments, whether truthful or apocryphal, has been so often related that it need not be repeated here. Hugh Dunn, as already stated, was one of the four patentees of the township. He appears to have been a prominent citizen. Of his ministerial work nothing is definitely known. It is probable that, gifted with exhortation and aptness to teach, he had been chosen by his brethren in connection with his associates, Drake and Dunning, to preside at such religious meetings as were held in the settlement, and, as opportunity offered, to preach the Gospel. We know but little of him subsequent to the formation of the Church, of the place or time of his death. The same name yet stands on the Church Register, one of the name being an honored deacon. Nor can it be doubted that a large part of the citizens of East Jersey and else-were of the same name are descendants either of Hugh Dunn or of his near relatives in Colonial times.

As we now take up the name of John Drake, the history of the Church from his time onward will be treated in sections corresponding with the terms of the pastorates.

JOHN DRAKE, First Pastor.
1689-1739.

This gentleman was chosen as pastor of the Church at the time of its organization and was then ordained, the Rev T. Killingsworth officiating. Mr. Drake, as we have seen, was one of the early settlers, having come into the province in 1668. His native place was Devonshire, Eng., the home of Sir Francis Drake, of whom he is supposed, not without good reason, to have been a nephew. Morgan Edwards[1] speaks of him as "an excellent man," a fact that his long pastorate would of itself indicate. The same authority mentions a "report" in his time, but without making any comments upon it, that the Church remained without change either by diminution or addition, from the

---

1. Rev. Morgan Edwards, born in 1722, died in 1795. Author of "Materials towards a History of New Jersey Baptists," &c.

time of its constitution till 1709, just twenty years ! How does such a report consist with the fact that thirteen of its members went out from it to form the Sabbatarian Church, near New Market, in 1705 ? Here was a diminution of thirteen within sixteen years of its existence, and of course there must have been an addition to the original number of six. The report is absolutely baseless. What is probably true is that after the lapse of twenty years from its formation, the Church numbered only twenty members. Let such a report, so unworthy the ministry of the "excellent" John Drake and so inconsistent with known facts, be forever laid to rest as a mere fiction of a hundred years ago.

In 1707 the Church united with four others in forming the Philadelphia Association, the first formed Baptist Association in America. The other four were those at Pennepek, Pa.; Middletown, N. J.; Cohansey, N. J., and Welch Tract, Del. It appears from the Century Minutes of the Association, that the churches had been accustomed to hold annually what were called " general meetings," with the design of concentrating evangelical efforts in and near the locality of the churches. The pastors attending these general meetings would, in their talk about Zion, very naturally report the spiritual condition of their respective churches and consult one another in regard to Christian doctrine, especially, in regard to questions of discipline of a perplexing character. Hence arose the desirableness of a yearly association, involving a representation of the churches by delegates, that the light and wisdom of such a body might be reflected on all the churches. To the Church at Pennepek, however, belongs the honor of having proposed such a body, as appears from the following record taken from their minutes: " Before our general meeting, held in Philadelphia in the 7th month, 1707, it was concluded by the several congregations of our judgment to make choice of some particular brethren, such as they thought most capable in every congregation, and those to meet at the yearly meeting, to consult about such things as were wanting in the churches, and to set them in order ; and these brethren, meeting at the said yearly meeting which began the 27th of the seventh month, on the seventh day of the week, agreed to continue the meeting till the third day following in the work of the public ministry." This record is deemed worthy of a place in this historical narrative, not only as an interesting item in itself, but as showing the origin of the first Association in this country, aptly called the " Mother of us all," and, still further, as defining the limited scope of such a body at that early period. It was simply a consulting and advisory body, the gathering of statistics not being at that time contemplated.[1]

The worthy pastor of this Church was deemed by his ministerial brethren and by the Church, capable of advising about such things as were wanting in the churches. At the session of 1712 we find his name among the members of a large committee " to hear and determine concerning a disturbance and rupture in the Church at Philadelphia and Pennepek." At the session of 1730 this Church sent up a request " for the help of ministering brethren at their general meeting." The Association " judged it necessary that our ministering brethren do supply such general meetings ; nevertheless, we, not knowing who, or or how to bind any of them, think it necessary that the church where such are held, send to them, that, if possible, they may be certain of some help." At the session of 1731 the Church was not represented. Twenty-one delegates were present from other churches. We find, however, this suggestive and sad item :   " The Association had neither queries nor requests from any of the churches ; but the associated brethren, seeing no messengers from Piscataway as usual, and hearing by some of our brethren of the sad and distracted condition of that congregation, they thought proper to write to them, and to appoint Mr. Jenkins Jones[2] and Mr. Joseph Eaton[3] to give them a visit before the winter, which by the blessing of God proved a means to reduce that Church to peace and order." This last item accounts, doubtless, for the urgent request of the Church at the session of the preceding year for ministerial help at their general meeting.   But how shall we account for " the sad and distracted condition of the Church ?" We learn from Dr. Benedict[4] that there came into the parish from Rhode Island a man calling himself Joseph Loveall—said to be an assumed name—bearing a letter of introduction signed by James Clark, Daniel Wightman and John Comer, all well known and worthy pastors of that Province, who certified that they then " knew nothing but that his conduct was agreeable to the Gospel of Christ." This man was gifted as a speaker, and as the Church, owing to the advanced age of Mr. Drake, wished to secure an assistant for him, they called Mr. Loveall, all too hastily, to ordination. Very soon after his ordination he was found to be grossly immoral, and was not allowed to administer the ordinances or to perform any pastoral duties.   He must, however, have had

1. No statistics appear in the Century Minutes until 1761, a period of over fifty years.
2. Pastor of Pennepek Church.
3. Pastor of Montgomery Church.
4. History, vol. 1, p. 567, and vol. 2, p. 15.

some sympathising friends who would neither believe him to be guilty nor allow the Church to exclude him; otherwise the distracted condition of the congregation can scarcely be explained. There are always those who are loth to believe that a man of brilliant talents and pleasing address can, like Satan, transform himself into an angel of light. He went from here to Maryland and thence to Virginia, in both of which Provinces he formed pastoral connections; and in the latter was excluded for the same iniquities that had been discovered in him here. The condition of things in the parish must, for the time being, have been very grievious to the venerable pastor. But, happily for him and the cause, the visits of his brethren, Jones and Eaton, served to restore peace and harmony to the Church. Mr. Drake's name appears on the Associational roll of messengers, for the last time in 1734. He was now advanced in years, and a journey to Philadelphia was no light undertaking in his time even for a man in the vigor of life, the road or roads leading thereto being scarcely worthy of the name. Mr. Drake continued in charge of the Church until 1739 when he entered into rest. And it may be added that no man knoweth of his sepulchre at this day. No stone or mark exists to tell where his body was laid. But his and our Redeemer knows,

> "And often from the skies
> Looks down and watches all his dust,
> Till He shall bid it rise."

Mr. Drake, according to Morgan Edwards, was thrice married. The names of his children were Isaac, Abraham, Francis, John, Benjamin, Samuel, Sarah and Rebecca. The daughters married into the families of the Hills and Randolphs. Unable to trace the family genealogy minutely, suffice it to state that Mr. William M. Drake and his brother, George Drake, so well known to us all, are the seventh generation in descent from George Drake, the brother of the first pastor, and the farm now owned by Mr. William M. Drake has been owned by successive generations of Drakes from the time it was first purchased when the territory was yet a wilderness. The late Mrs. Henry Smalley was a lineal descendant of the Rev. John Drake.

BENJAMIN STELLE, SECOND PASTOR.

1739-1759.

The Rev. Benjamin Stelle was a son of Poincet or Pontius Stelle, a native of the South of France, who, as one of the oppressed Hugenots, sought refuge in America and settled in New York. There Benjamin was born in 1693. His mother's name was Eugenie Legereaux Stelle.

About the year 1707 he came to Piscataway. The time of his uniting with the Church is unknown. He married Miss Mercy Drake. His name first appears in the Associational list of delegates in 1729, ten years before Mr. Drake's death. We meet with it again in the lists of 1733, '35, '39, '40, '42, '44, and for the last time in that of 1746. He may have attended other sessions, the names of delegates not appearing in all the minutes. The time of his license is also unknown. But from his moral and Christian worth and his high standing as a citizen, it was quite probable that he was called by his brethren to preach the Word and render assistance to the venerable Drake in the last years of his ministry. But of this there is no certain record. He was not ordained till after Mr. Drake's death. He was then no novice, being at least 55 years of age. Held in high esteem by his fellow citizens, offices of honor and trust had been thrust upon him. He was a Justice of the Peace, a chosen Freeholder for ten consecutive years, a Collector of Taxes from 1727–1731, and Overseer of Roads after as well as before his ordination. His election to these various offices speaks loudly for the sagacity and moral worth of the citizens of that day in seeking to fill these offices with men of integrity and ability. It speaks volumes for the man who could discharge all these civic functions without compromising his character as a consistent Christian and a good minister of Jesus Christ. Honored as Mr. Stelle was by the people, he was still more honored by the Great Head of the Church, who, in his grace, made him a winner of souls and an upbuilder of the saints. During his pastorate the Church largely increased in numbers and influence, numbering in 1746 over one hundred members. These members were not all in Piscataway, but scattered over a wide extent of country. Fifteen of the members[1] living in the vicinity of Plainfield and Scotch Plains, were on September 8, 1747, constituted an independent Baptist Church at Scotch Plains, of which the Rev. Benjamin Miller, a native of Piscataway, and also a licentiate of this Church, took the spiritual oversight in February, 1748. This Church, the eighth one organized in New Jersey, united with the Philadelphia Association the same year. The wisdom of organizing this new interest soon became apparent. Small in the beginning, the divine blessing so largely rested on the labors of the devout and zealous Miller that after the lapse of

1. Their names were William Darby, Recompense Stanbery, John Lambert, John Dennis, John Stanbery, Henry Crosley, John Sutton, Jr., Isaac Manning, Mary Brodwell, Mary Green, Mary Dennis, Tibiah Sutton, Catherine Manning, Sarah DeCamp, Sarah Pearce. The letter dismissory is signed by Benjamin Stelle, Benjamin Miller, Isaac Stelle, James Pyatt, John Clarkson, Thomas Worthington, Thomas A. Martin and John Drake. This letter bears the date of August 5, 1747.

fifteen years from its recognition it reported to the Association one hundred and forty-four members, or, more than three times the membership of the mother church for that year.

In the year 1752, another band of members living in and near Morristown, some twenty-five miles distant from Piscataway, were duly set apart as an independent Church.[1]   Their first pastor was Rev. John Gano, whose interesting life is well told by Dr. Benedict.[2]   From this time on we know but little of the life or labors of the much revered Benjamin Stelle, only that he continued in the pastoral relation up to the time of his death in January, 1759, in the 76th year of his age, and the twentieth of his pastorate.   As a pastor he had fed the flock and welcomed lambs to the fold.   Zealous for the triumph of truth and for the glory of the Master, he had seen two colonies go out from the Church, yet comparatively small in numbers, to plant the standard of his and their Lord in other fields, and therein he rejoiced.   While in his prime, before "age stole fire from his mind, and vigor from his limbs," he was regarded by his contemporaries as "a popular preacher" and a man without reproach.   And although years before his death his head became "frosted o'er with time" we do not learn, either through record or tradition, that the Church grew weary of his ministry and wished him to vacate the field.   On the contrary, they clung to him to the last, as one justly entitled to their veneration and love.   His remains were buried in the old graveyard at Piscatawaytown.   An ordinary headstone, erected to his memory, bears this simple inscription :

In Memory of

THE REV. BENJAMIN STELLE,

Minister

OF THE BAPTIST SOCIETY

in Piscataway,

Who departed this life Jan. 22, 1759.

Ætat 76.

———

Your Fathers, where are they ? And
the Prophets, do they live
forever ?—Zech. 1:5.

Mr. Stelle left a large family, the genealogy of which will appear at the close of our narrative.

---

1.   The names of the constituents were : Daniel Sutton, Jonas Goble, John Sutton, Malatiah Goble, Jemima Wiggins, Daniel Walling, Ichabod Tompkins, Sarah Wiggins, Mary Goble, Naomi Allen and Robert Goble.

2.   Vol. II, pp. 306-323.

ISAAC STELLE, THIRD PASTOR.

1759-1781.

Rev. Isaac Stelle, son of Benjamin and Mercy Stelle, was born in Piscataway in 1719. He married Miss Christiana Clarkson. He was ordained as assistant to his father in 1751, and became sole pastor of the Church after his father's death in 1759. What his educational advantages had been, we know not, but he appears to have been a man of more than ordinary vigor and sprightliness of mind; a peer among his fellows, and from the first able to hold a conspicuous position among his brethren in the ministry, and a large place in their hearts. Morgan Edwards speaks of "the goodness of the man and the excellency of his preaching. Dr. Samuel Jones, in his century sermon, after referring to the earlier and more eminent ministers of the Association, adds that "a junior class came forward in the churches who were in a pretty high degree eminent in their day; as John Davies, of Hartford; Robert Kelsie, of Cohansey; Peter Peterson VanHorn, of Lower Dublin; Isaac Eaton, of Hopewell; Mr. Walton, of Morristown; Isaac Stelle, of Piscataway; Benjamin Miller, of Scotch Plains, and John Gano, of New York. These were burning and shining lights, especially the last three. May the God of Elijah grant that a double portion of their spirit may rest on all that stand as watchmen on Zion's walls." A pardonable pride may be indulged that two of these "especially burning and shining lights" were licentiates of this Church, namely: Benjamin Miller and Isaac Stelle.

In the Association Mr. Stelle was highly esteemed for his wisdom, sound judgment, and pulpit gifts. He was often placed on important committees, and appointed to represent the Association in sister bodies, in Rhode Island, Connecticut, New York and Virginia. He preached the introductory sermon before the Association in 1752, again in 1759; also in 1766, from John, 1:14: "The Word was made flesh, and dwelt among us (and we behold his glory, the glory of the only begotten of the Father) full of grace and truth"; and for the last time in 1774, from Jeremiah, 23: 28: "The prophet that hath a dream, let him tell a dream; and he that hath my word, let him speak my word faithfully; what is the chaff to the wheat? saith the Lord." He was chosen Moderator of the Association in 1776, and again in 1780. In the year 1763 he wrote by appointment the Circular Letter; or, Pastoral Address to the churches, and again in 1768. A part of the former we here transcribe, believing it will be read with interest by the members of the Church, the more, as in all probability he left no manuscript sermons or other document whereby may be indicated the character of his mind and the fervor of his zeal :

"The elders and messengers of the several Baptist congregations in Pennsylvania and provinces adjacent, now met in general Association at Philadelphia, the 11th, 12th and 13th of October, 1763.

To THE SEVERAL CHURCHES WE REPRESENT, SEND CHRISTIAN SALUTATION :

DEARLY BELOVED BRETHREN :—We have the satisfaction to acquaint you of our meeting together, according to appointment. A good measure of brotherly love has subsisted among us during the time of our consultation. Thanks be to the Lord who is wisdom and counsel to his people.

And now, brethren, receive a word of exhortation in love. Strive to abound in vital piety ; see that you walk worthy of the vocation wherewith you are called. Be careful to maintain a steady course of cheerful obedience to God all the days of your life. Neglect not prayer, neither family nor closet. Strengthen the hands of your ministers and encourage their visits to vacant places. Delight yourselves in the Word, worship and ordinances of God. Make the sacred oracles the rule of all your actions. Learn by Christ's sermon on the Mount, to forgive your enemies; strive to live peaceably with all men.

May you ever be able to walk together in the unity of the Spirit, provoking one another to love and good works, and that being by promise united to an inheritance among them that are sanctified, you may at last hear the voice of the heavenly bridegroom say unto you, 'Come up hither'; which may God, of his infinite mercy, grant for Jesus sake. Amen."

All these exhortations might be as pertinently addressed to the churches now as to those of a hundred and twenty-five years ago. Notice, particularly his interest in evangelical work, in the counsel, "Strengthen the hands of your ministers, and *encourage their visits to vacant places.*"

In the Association that met at New York in 1772, during which Mr. Isaac Skillman was set apart to the ministry, Mr. Stelle, with Rev. Abel Morgan and Rev. John Gano, performed the ordination service after a sermon by President Manning. At the ordination of Dr. Manning himself ten years before at Scotch Plains, we are told by Prof. Guild that " his beloved friend, the Rev. Isaac Stelle, of Piscataway, made the ordaining prayer." Between Dr. Manning and Mr. Stelle there subsisted a close and loving intimacy until the death of the latter. In President Manning's diary of a journey from Providence to Philadelphia and return in 1779,[1]

1. See Prof. Guild's "Manning and Brown University," pp. 266-286, a very valuable and interesting memoir. The diary or journal alone abounds in historical incidents, and also in allusion to persons and families so well known then in this section, as are their descendants now, that it would well repay every Baptist living between Elizabeth and Hopewell to read.

he refers repeatedly to Mr. Stelle, whom he met first during this journey at Scotch Plains, and where both of them preached on the 6th day of June; whom he visited July 18, and for whom he preached twice. "Called on him on the 23d. He was not at home, met him at Mr. Hall's in Brunswick. August 22, preached at the Plains with Mr. Stelle who preached at 6 o'clock at Morristown." This was their final meeting on earth. Another of Mr. Stelle's contemporaries and his bosom friend was the Rev. Benjamin Miller, the first pastor of the daughter Church at Scotch Plains. Morgan Edwards, in referring to the intimacy of Mr. Miller and Mr. Stelle, speaks of Mr. Miller as Mr. Stelle's "other self." Both, inspired with zeal for mission work, made long journeys together to remote parts of the country, once as far South as Virginia, preaching as they went, visiting feeble Churches, and everywhere testifying the Gospel of the grace of God. Such itinerant labors were rare even in that age, and bear witness to the self-denial of these good men and their consecration to the Master's work.[1]

It would interesting to know much more of the life and labors of the third pastor, even to form some idea by pen or pencil of his personal appearance; but, as no portrait remains of him or of his predecessors, we are prepared to accept what Prof. Guild says of him: "He possessed a temperament exceedingly active and a disposition uncommonly amiable." That he was a preacher far above mediocrity, is apparent from the prominence given him, by his contemporary brethren, in public bodies—brethren who, like him, adorned their holy profession and made their mark on the age; Miller, Edwards, Gano, Isaac Eaton, Abel Morgan, and others of whom the world was not worthy. He and Miller, who illustrated the friendship of David and Jonathan, both died the same year, Mr. Stelle, October 9, Mr. Miller, November 14, 1781. "Lovely and pleasant," says one, "were they in their lives, and in death they were not long divided, the one having survived the other only thirty-five days."

"If one was grieved, it did them both annoy,
If one rejoiced, the other felt the joy;
When one was gone, the other could not stay,
But quickly hastened to eternal day."

Mr. Stelle did not attain to the venerable ages of his predecessors, being scarcely sixty-three years old when the Lord called him to rest from his labors. But his works followed with him, to be, with him, held in everlasting remembrance. His pastorate covered twenty-two years,

1. President Manning, in his letter to Rev. Benjamin Wallin, of London, under date of May 23, 1783, informs him of the death of "two eminent Baptist ministers nearly two years ago—the Rev. Messrs. Miller and Stelle, of the Scotch Plains and Piscataway Churches."—*M. and B. U.,* p. 295.

his entire ministry twenty-nine years, and, excepting his occasional missionary tours and one or two visits to Rhode Island, were confined exclusively to this Church. In Piscataway he was born and born again, licensed and ordained. In Piscataway he lived, labored and died. His remains were placed by the side of his father's. The inscription on the stone reads:

In Memory of ye

REV. MR. ISAAC STELLE,

Baptist Minister of ye Gospel of Christ,

at Piscataway,

Who departed this life
Oct. ye 9th, 1781, in ye 63d year of his Age.

A loving Husband, a tender Parent and a
Friend to all that love ye
Lord Jesus.

No more ye Gospel Trumpet sounds
By him who had much given,
One in this Lower World imployed
But now imployed in Heaven.

Mr. Stelle left seven sons and two daughters. His son, Benjamin, graduated at Princeton in 1766, and soon after established a Latin School at Providence, which was largely patronized. It was a daughter of this gentleman who became the second wife of the Hon. Nicholas Brown, the distinguished benefactor of Brown University. Mr. Stelle was also Clerk of the Baptist Church in Providence for many years.

The descendants of the Rev. Benjamin and Rev. Isaac Stelle are spread over all the country. They are in our chief cities and in country places, occupying the marts of business, or engaged in husbandry and manufactures, or pursuing various professional callings. Their influence in this Church from the beginning, and in the Baptist Israel at large, is not to be estimated in time. May all that bear the name, as they multiply through future generations, be in no wise unworthy of their honored ancestors.

Before we proceed further in our narrative, let us pause and consider where we are in history. It is the month of October, 1781, nearly a century after the planting of the Church—an eventful and sad month in its history, and still more eventful and joyous month in the history of our nation. Isaac Stelle rests from his labors and receives his crown. Ten days afterwards the month witnesses to the last blow struck for American independence at Yorktown, and the surrender of Lord Cornwallis and his army, to an end of the toils, sacrifices and sufferings of the patriot army and people, and to the rejoicings and thanksgivings that begin in the victorious army and spread throughout the Union.

No part of our country had suffered more than New Jersey, not only from the tread of armed hosts to and fro, and battles fought on her soil, but from the terrorism and robbery of marauding bands of British soldiers and from the insolence and destructiveness of their allies, the tories, of whom this part of the State had its full share. Few dwellings, few church edifices, in this region escaped pillage. Few were the farms that were not robbed of their stock and of whatever could minister either to the greed or revengeful spirit of these plundering bands.

Now all is changed. Peace begins to dawn. The nation feels that it *must* come, that its blessings are just at hand. Under the influence of these anticipations—soon to be realized—the people begin to be of good cheer. East Jersey, no longer ground between the upper and nether millstones of British oppression and tory vandalism, lifts up her bowed head and gratefully hails a new era of national and religious life. This Church, the members of which had borne their full proportion of privation and sufferings and had experienced with other churches the evils of declension in religion and vital piety, we find still holding on its way and gathering together for worship and mutual counsel and exhortation, though reduced in numbers.

As already stated the minutes that have survived the Revolution begin on the 29th day of August, 1781, and are called the "Minutes of the First-Day Baptist Church at Piscataway." It might be supposed that at this meeting, or one held soon afterwards, there would be some allusion to the great loss the Church had sustained in the destruction or theft of its minutes for the preceding hundred years, but there is not the slightest allusion to so deplorable a fact. [1] But in strict harmony with the aim of the Church doubtless from the beginning, certainly for the last century, namely, to maintain the purity of the Church, its first "proceedings" relate to three delinquent members. The next meeting for business is held in October[2] of the same year, and opposite the numeral 9, in the margin, we meet with this brief statement: "Our much esteemed pastor, Rev. Isaac Stelle, departed this life." Nothing more. How much it would gratify us to know more—to know how the death of such a man, minister, pastor, affected the Church and congregation ; to know which of his brethren officiated at his funeral, and sought to extol the grace that had made him the devoted servant of his Lord that he was, and one of the most useful men of the age.

1. Church records in those days were kept with—it might almost be said - provoking brevity.

2. The Church meetings were then held bi-monthly.

For some unexplained reason the "proceedings" of the Church between October 31, 1781, and May 26, 1784, are not recorded. But, from a marginal note, we infer that it did meet, perhaps at irregular intervals, and took into consideration the call of a successor to Rev. Isaac Stelle. That note reads: "November, 1783, Rev. Reune Runyon became pastor of this Church." Thus are we brought down to the life and times of the fourth pastor.

REUNE RUNYON, Fourth Pastor.
1783–1811.

This gentleman was a son of Reune Runyon, Esq., who, like the Stelles, was of French extraction.[1] The Runyons came into the township in 1676, but how many and from whence they immediately came, cannot be definitely ascertained. It is, however, known that the great grandfather of Rev. Reune Runyon,[2] viz: Vincent Runyon, was of the province of Poitou, or Portiers, France, and tradition states that he and others of the same name were Huguenots who, to escape persecution, went first to the Isle of Jersey and thence came to East Jersey in 1676. Reune Runyon married Miss Rachel Drake. Their son, Reune Runyon, was born in Piscataway, November 29, 1741. In 1765 he married Miss Anne Bray. He was licensed to preach in 1771, and in June, 1782, he was ordained as pastor of the church at Morristown, and continued in that relation about eleven years, embracing the period of the Revolutionary war, during the great part of which the house of worship there was used as a military hospital and storehouse. The meetings of the Church were necessarily suspended and its members scattered. Yet was the pastor accounted faithful, and through his labors about twenty souls were added to the Church. He was the fourth pastor of that Church, the first one having been the eminent John Gano.[3] In the month of November, 1783, he entered upon pastoral duties here. The Church promised him £50 per annum, which, it was said, was not always promptly paid; but, as he owned a good farm he obtained from it a comfortable support for a large family. His ministry proved a rich blessing to the Church, which, at the time of his settlement, numbered only forty persons. Two only were added the following

1. The name was originally spelled "Rongnion," or "Rongneon."
2. See Genealogical Table at the close of this History.
3. Mr. Gano married a daughter of John Stites, Esq., Mayor of Elizabethtown, and a ruling elder of the Scotch Plains Church. Miss Stites was a sister of President Manning's wife. Mr. Gano was pastor, after leaving Morristown, of the Church in New York about twenty-five years, except when acting as chaplain in the army. He removed to Kentucky in 1787 and there died at a good old age.

year ; none the next year. The whole number reported to the Association in 1785 was thirty-nine. The year 1786 was a year of special grace
and large prosperity to this and other churches in the State,[1] twenty-eight
being reported to the Association as having been baptised in that year,
making the whole membership one hundred and twenty-one. This
revival continued many months, twenty-two baptisms being reported the
next year, the total membership reaching, in 1790, one hundred and forty-
eight, or nearly four-fold that of 1785.

In the early part of Mr. Runyon's pastorate he was not *ex-officio*,
Moderator of meetings for business. He may, possibly have declined
to preside for prudential reasons, there being then some delicate matters
before the Church which should, in his opinion, be determined by the
independent judgment of the brethren. Be this as it may, at the meeting of May 26, 1784, it was "Resolved, That for the future on days of
business, it shall be the practice of this Church at the opening of the
business of the day to choose a Moderator."[2] Most generally Deacon
Edward Griffith[3] was chosen to preside. The custom of choosing a
Moderator at each meeting for business was observed for many years.
It was discontinued at the settlement of the seventh pastor when it was
"Resolved, That Brother Lewis be chosen as our Standing Moderator."

In the year 1789 the question that had long been agitated among
Baptists, and concerning which the churches differed in sentiment and
practice, namely: whether deacons should be ordained by imposition
of hands, came under discussion in this Church, and by a formal vote
was decided in the negative. It was destined, however, to come up
again, as will presently appear.

In the month of August, 1791, a communication was received from
the Scotch Plains Church requesting this Church " to consider the propriety of holding meetings two-thirds of the Lord's days at Samptown,
steadily for one year, to be conducted by Rev. Reune Runyon and
Rev. William Van Horne.[4] After the appointment of a joint committee by the two churches which met at Samptown the same year and
brought their combined wisdom to bear on the whole matter, the result
was the recognition of the members living in the neighborhood of

---

1. Middletown reported 25 baptised; Scotch Plains, 47 ; New York, 41; Mt. Bethel,
76; Morristown,27 ; Hightstown, 66.
2. This resolution justifies the inference that heretofore the pastors had been
Moderators, *ex-officio*.
3. This good deacon was the maternal ancestor of the esteemed and well-known Dr.
E. M. Hunt, now of Trenton.
4. The successor to Rev. Benjamin Miller, the first pastor. He served the Church
twenty two years and then started for Ohio, intending to reside there, but died on the
way at Pittsburg in 1807, aged 61 years.

Samptown as an independent Church in the year 1792. As a majority
of the constituent members were dismissed by the Scotch Plains Church,
the Samptown Church must be regarded as a daughter of that Church.

As a matter of interest connected with this event, it may be stated
that the removal of the meeting-house to that neighborhood had been
mooted by some members of the Church, and so intent were they in
having it done that they offered a motion in a business meeting held
in February, 1791, "that our meeting-house be moved to Samptown."
Strange as it may seem, the minutes do not inform us how this motion
was decided. But we know it *was* decided, and only as a people "having
understanding of the times, to know what Israel ought to do" could
have decided it.

The year 1792 is also memorable for the withdrawal of the Church
from the Philadelphia Association, after a union with it of eighty-five
years, and for greater convenience, uniting with the New York Association, for which purpose it had been dismissed by the mother body the
previous year. Mr. Runyon was Moderator of the New York Association in the years 1797, 1801, 1803 and 1808. At the session of 1810
he preached the introductory sermon from Hebrews, 12:2, "Looking
unto Jesus," etc. He was honored among his brethren. The condition of the Church from 1793 through several subsequent years,
though one of peace and harmony, was not one of growth. In 1794 it
appointed a day of fasting and prayer, and again in the following year,
in accordance with the recommendation of the Association to all the
churches, it observed four days of public prayer "on account of the
coldness and barrenness in the affairs of religion." There were additions until 1807 when, in that and several successive years, numbers
were baptized, in all nearly fifty persons. Mr. Runyon's pastorate
ended only with his life. After a tedious illness, which he bore with
patient resignation sustained by "a good hope through grace," he
entered into rest November 21, 1811, aged seventy years. The length of
his pastorate was twenty-eight years, of his entire ministry nearly forty
years. The Church, at the time of his death, numbered one hundred
and forty-nine, a higher number than it had ever before reached. That
he was a faithful pastor and careful to maintain the discipline of the
Church, let the following resolutions, passed early in his pastorate, doubtless with his sanction if not at his instigation, testify:

"RESOLVED, That our stated meetings of business shall be attended
by every male member, and, any neglecting, without being able to show
cause, shall be deemed blameable and ought to be reproved."

We yield to the temptation to quote another resolution of April 27, 1788:

"RESOLVED, That no one member speak to any matter without rising up, and not more than thrice to any one particular, except on leave of the Moderator then acting."

Other items of interest during the ministry of Mr. Runyon will be hereafter referred to under their appropriate headings. As already stated, Mr. Runyon had a large family. His descendants and those of his ancestors are to be found all over our land. The name has been on the Church Register, probably from near the beginning, certainly for the last hundred years. One of this name is now a deacon, another is Clerk of the Church. Nearly a score of others are on the Register.

Mr. Runyon's remains were interred in the old graveyard at Piscatawaytown hard by those of his predecessors. The inscription on his headstone reads:

Sacred to the Memory of
THE REV. REUNE RUNYON,
Who died Nov. 21, 1811,
In the 71st year of his Age.

My flesh shall slumber in the ground
Till the last trumpet's joyful sound ;
Then burst the chains with sweet surprise,
And in my Savior's image rise.

The following great grandchildren of Rev. Reune Runyon are now members of the Baptist churches:

Piscataway Church.—Mr. and Mrs. George Drake, Mr. William Drake, Mr. and Mrs. Jonathan Dayton, Mr. William Dayton, Mr. Isaac Dayton, Mrs. Henry Brantingham, Mrs. Mefford Runyon, Mrs. Samuel S. Dayton.

New Brooklyn.—Mr. Jesse Dayton, Mrs. Ephraim Boice, Mr. Reune B. Manning, Mr. William Manning, Mrs. Manning Randolph.

First Plainfield.—Mr. Samuel R. Manning, Miss Gussie Runyon.

New Market.—Mr. John Dayton, Mrs. Peter Benward, Mr. Simeon Dayton, Mrs. Lewis Walker, Miss Laura J. Runyon.

JAMES McLAUGHLIN, FIFTH PASTOR.
1812–1817.

After an interval of nine months from the death of Mr. Runyon, Rev. James McLaughlin was unanimously called to the pastorate, and began his labors October 1, 1812. Mr. McLaughlin was born in 1768 and was baptized in Wilmington by Rev. Philip Hughes in 1784, and was probably a licentiate of the Church in that place. He was ordained in 1789 as pastor of the Hilltown, Pa., Church, where he remained until 1805. From 1806 to 1809 he was at Flemington ; in the year 1810 at Burlington, and at Kingwood in 1811, from which place he came to this field.

The Church having no parsonage at the time of Mr. McLaughlin's settlement, he rented a House in New Brunswick where a number of the members lived, and for whose accommodation and more direct Gospel effort in that place, a house of worship had been built two years before. The New Brunswick brethren had united in perfect harmony with the Church in the call to Mr. McLaughlin. He preached in the Piscataway meeting-house in the morning and in the New Brunswick house in the afternoon on Lord's days. The members in New Brunswick, twenty-three in number, were, on September 21, 1816, recognized as an independent Church.[1] Mr. McLaughlin supplied the Church at New Brunswick till the following May (1817) when, owing to its desire to have the exclusive services of a pastor he terminated his connection with it, and a few months afterwards, October 9, 1817, resigned the pastorate of the mother Church, having served it just five years. During these years the Church was not favored with many additions, the minutes recording only eleven baptisms. The total number of members reported to the Association in the year 1818 was one hundred and thirteen. The decrease is to be attributed chiefly to the large numbers dismissed to form the Church at New Brunswick. The late Deacon Samuel Smith, in his reminiscences of former pastors in an unpublished manuscript of twenty years ago or more, describes Mr. McLaughlin as "a man of eminent piety, a good minister of Jesus Christ, grave in his deportment, and unusually solemn in pulpit address." The memory of his many virtues and faithful labors is still tenderly cherished by the few yet remaining of those who are contemporary with him in the Church. On leaving here Mr. McLaughlin became pastor of the Second Baptist Church in Philadelphia ; in 1826 of the New Britain Church, Pa. He died in Lambertville, N. J., August 19, 1827, aged fifty-nine years, and was buried in the graveyard of the Second Baptist Church of Hopewell. The late Mrs. G. S. Webb, so much beloved by all who knew her, was a daughter of Mr. McLaughlin.

1. The names of these constituent members were Asa Runyon, Elizabeth Runyon, Joseph Runyon, Sarah Runyon, Sarah L. Dunham, Sarah Post, Ruth Branon, Henry Wright, Richard C. Runyon, Phoebe Runyon, Sarah Corkins, Sarah Merrill, Sarah Ayres, Squire Martin, Susannah Martyn, William Potts, Esther Potts, Richard Lupardus, Charlotte Lupardus, Sarah Probasco, Sarah Kent, Abigail Coon, Mary Vansyele.

DANIEL DODGE, Sixth Pastor.
1818–1832.

Mr. Dodge, whose parents were natives of Massachusetts, was born in Annapolis Royal, Nova Scotia, in 1775. Of his early life we know but little. At the age of eighteen we find him at Woodstock, Vt., and there and then consecrating himself to Christ and uniting with the Baptist Church under the charge of Rev. Elisha Ransom. In 1797, at the age of twenty-two, having been licensed to preach, he traveled as far south as Maryland and Virginia, and after preaching in various places he was ordained in 1801 in Anne Arundel County, Md. The next year he became pastor of the Church at Wilmington where for nearly seventeen years he labored abundantly, the Lord working with him and crowning his labors with a rich harvest of souls. While there he baptised two hundred and fifty-nine converts. His name is pronounced with reverence and his memory is fragrant there to this day.

He entered upon pastoral duties here October 1, 1818, on a salary of $600 per annum. He was now about forty-three years old, in the full vigor of his intellectual and physical powers, ripe in Christian and ministerial experience, thoroughly established in the doctrines of the Gospel and as firm as a rock in maintaining them.

Mr. Dodge, like his predecessor, lived in New Brunswick. The divine blessing attended his labors, preeminently during the first three years of his ministry, nearly sixty souls having been baptized and added to the Church within that time. And no succeeding year passed without the accession of one or more by baptism. Eighteen were baptized in the last year of his ministry here. Nevertheless, fidelity to history compels us to record that the Church never passed through a more troublous and painful period than that covered by the first nine years of Mr. Dodge's pastorate, not because of any moral or ministerial shortcomings in him, nor because he did not conscientiously seek the edification and prosperity of the Church, but because of a difference of sentiment or opinion between him and a number of prominent members regarding Church polity, and the lawfulness or unlawfulness of marrying a deceased wife's sister. Mr. Dodge held, and had held before his settlement here, that "the laying on of hands after baptism was a Gospel ordinance and necessary to be practiced."[1] This was contrary to the practice of the Church, that form having been laid aside more than thirty years.[2] Its reintroduction was

1. Quoted from the old Minutes.
2. Old Minutes, p. 66. It thus appears that the laying on of hands after baptism had been, *in a former time*, the practice of the Church.

grievous to certain brethren. The difficulty was finally compromised by leaving to the option of the candidate whether to be received with or without the imposition of hands.

The question whether deacons should be ordained also came under discussion; first, at a church meeting held in May, 1820, at which time the pastor spoke strongly in favor of their ordination. No decision of the question being reached, the discussion was resumed in November following and closed with the adoption of the following resolution :

"RESOLVED, That notwithstanding the practice of ordaining deacons had been abandoned by a decision of the Church in 1789, we dissent from that decision, and agree that it is a practice fully authorized by Scripture and ought to be adhered to."

In accordance with this resolution we find under date of June 2, 1821, this item : " Peter Runyon, John F. Randolph and William F. Manning were this day ordained deacons by the prayers and laying on of the hands of Elders Jacob Randolph, Daniel Dodge and G. S. Webb."[1] Thus this vexed question was, for the time being, laid to rest.

The marriage question was not so easily disposed of, and for a long time it greatly disquieted the Church. In 1827 the Church sent up to the Association this query : " Whether the Scriptures did not prohibit marriage between a man and a sister of his deceased wife ?" As the Association gave no direct answer to the query, but simply left it " for each Church to determine the lawfulness of such marriage in the light of the Holy Scriptures," the Church at Samptown renewed the query the following year. This was referred to a committee of seven, Elder Parkinson, Chairman, who reported at the same session that " though they were unanimously and decidedly of the opinion that there is nothing in the Holy Scriptures forbidding such marriages, nevertheless, considering the importance of the question and its bearings on the Christian and civil community, they advised the appointment of a committee of three to prepare a more full report upon the subject at the next term." From this opinion Elder Dodge, who was Moderator, expressed his " solemn dissent, as tending, in his belief, to sanction incest." This committee of three having failed to present such report, the following year (1829) the Association " cordially and affectionately recommended to the churches not to make a difference of opinion respecting the matter in question any bar to Christian fellowship and friendly intercourse between them, to an exchange of pastoral labor, or to the mutual dismission and reception of members." It appears that this judicious advice

1. Old Minutes, p. 73.

had not been practically anticipated by this Church. Controversy on the question waxed more and more warm and resulted in alienations and divisions. By request of the Church, presented at the session last named, a Council, consisting of seven persons, was appointed by the Association to aid in the restoration of harmony to the Church. This Council, of which Elder Parkinson was Chairman, and A. R. Martin, Clerk, met with the Church on the 10th day of June, 1829,[1] and after a session of three days succeeded in healing every difficulty and effecting a formal reconciliation between the Church and its disaffected members. At the same time (June 12, 1829), and in accordance with the advice of the Council, the Church voted that "in future, candidates be received exclusively by the imposition of hands."

None can doubt that the excellent pastor felt bound, by his own convictions of divine teaching, to take the course he did throughout this protracted controversy, however painful it was to a number of good and honored brethren. To establish all in what he believed to be the faith of the Gospel was his sincere and persistent aim—an aim from which no earthly considerations could make him swerve a hair's breadth. Men of positive convictions, united with the ability to advocate and urge them, have always been liable to the charge of obstinacy, and Mr. Dodge was not exempt from the charge. But in him it was not obstinacy, but rather the power of conscience urging him onward to the accomplishment of his purposes. It is not to be implied, however, that he was always faultless in spirit and word in his controversy with the minority part of the Church. To err is human, and the human was manifest in him. Yet was he one of the excellent of the earth, and so honored of God in his work that through all these years of controversy sinners were brought under the power of the truth and added to the Church, in all, one hundred and five souls.

Having noticed the passage of resolutions that involved painful discussion, we cannot pass by one that was introduced in the year following that of Mr. Dodge's settlement, which seems to have been unattended by any important discussion, although one of broad bearings even in this day. At a stated meeting of the Church held February 4, 1819, "Brother Peter Runyon observed that he was 'difficultied' in his mind because the Church debarred the sisters from voting in the church." The matter "was held over to our next stated meeting, for considera-

---

1. The Church appointed Mr. Dodge and eight others to attend the said Council and represent the Church in the investigation of the difficulties, as follows: Rev. Daniel Dodge, Peter Runyon, Isaac A. Stelle, William F. Manning, Justus Runyon, Daniel Runyon, Isaac Dayton, Jonathan Dayton, Benjamin Stelle.

tion whether they have a scriptural right in all cases to vote ; if not, in what cases they should have the privilege." At the next stated meeting held May 12, " it was carried by a large majority that the sisters have an equal right, in all cases with the brethren, in voting, speaking and governing the Church." It is a fair inference that this resolution met with the full concurrence of the pastor. Nor does it appear from the minutes that it has ever been rescinded.

Mr. Dodge remained with the Church three years after the meeting of the Council. Nothing occurred in the meantime to affect its peace and prosperity. Mr. Dodge purchased a farm [1] near the meeting-house and resided thereon till his resignation as pastor, which took effect August 29, 1832, when he was dismissed to the church at Newark to which he had been recently called. There we are told that he was eminent as a peacemaker—"restoring harmony and confidence among members."[2] During his ministry there of six years the membership increased from one hundred and twenty to two hundred and thirteen. From Newark he removed to Philadelphia, and from 1838 to 1850 he was pastor of the Second Church. He died in that city, May 13, 1851, in the triumphs of faith, respected and honored by all who knew him. He was a grand old man. Time and grace had mellowed his feelings and made him yet more beautiful and saintly in character. His goodly physique, his dignified carriage, his hoary head, his grave yet benign expression together with the recollection of his long and useful ministry commanded the loving and tender regard of his ministerial brethren who spontaneously assigned him the chief seat in Associational and other meetings, and, when he spoke, listened to his words as those of a man who walked with God, and in whom was the spirit of wisdom.

DANIEL LEWIS, Seventh Pastor.
1833–1849.

From the dismission of Mr. Dodge in October, '32, until the following June, the Church was without a pastor, though not destitute of supplies nor of candidates for the pulpit. The only item of interest recorded in the minutes previous to the election of a pastor was the setting apart of Mr. Drake Stelle as deacon by prayer and imposition of hands by Elder James.

---

1. Now owned and occupied by Nelson B. Runyon.
2. History of the Church, prepared by I. Peckham, published in Minutes of the East Jersey Association, 1876.

On the 23d day of June the Church extended a call to Rev. Daniel Lewis. This call was for one year, with the promise that he should receive all the funds accruing from the rent of pews. Before the year expired he was called for another year, on a salary of $400 and the pew rents. Both of these calls, limiting the pastoral relation to one year, were a departure from the usual practice of the Church. At the expiration of the second year the minutes contain no account of any action in regard to his continuance in the pastorate, probably because by this time the bonds between pastor and people had become so strong as to make both alike feel that nothing but death could break them, and that any formal action in the matter would be a work of supererogation.

Mr. Lewis was born in Barnstable, Mass., July, 21, 1777, married to Mary Dyer, May 13, 1798 ; ordained as pastor of the church at New Gloucester, Me. The Rev. Mr. Boardman, father of the distinguished missionary, George Dana Boardman, preached the ordination sermon. Subsequently he became pastor of churches at Ipswich, Mass., Providence, R. I., Fishkill, N.Y., Frankfort, Pa., Wilmington, Del., Patterson, N. J.,[1] lastly Piscataway.

When Mr. Lewis was called to this Church, it was found that he, also, was a man who had some opinions. His views respecting the imposition of hands after baptism being the reverse of those held by his esteemed predecessor, he objected decidedly to the practice and hesitated about accepting the call. Whereupon, in the month following (July 7), the Church met and rescinded its resolution of June 12, 1829, which forbade the reception of newly baptized persons except by the imposition of hands, and left the mode of reception to the option of the candidates.[2] This being satisfactory to Mr. Lewis he at once accepted the call and entered upon pastoral duties.

At a special meeting held January 1, 1834, it was also voted that the resolution passed August 29, 1827, respecting incestuous marriages,[3] be rescinded. It does not appear from the records of the Church that the motion to rescind met with any opposition or was even regarded as of questionable propriety. By these two motions, both secured by the

1. The dates of ordination and of pastorates (save that of Piscataway), cannot be given, Mr. Lewis's papers having been consumed in the great fire at Paterson.

2. Old Minutes, p 124.

3. The preamble and resolution read as follows :
" WHEREAS, There has been much disputation among the members of this Church on the subject of incestuous marriages, and a query by the Church having been presented to the Association for their advice, and the same returned unanswered and the matter left to each church to decide the case for themselves ; therefore, we—
RESOLVE, That all marriages that are within the fourth degree (in a direct line), either in consanguinity or affinity, are contrary to our Confession of Faith and the Holy Scriptures."—Old Minutes, p. 87.

influence of Mr. Lewis, the Church was brought back to its practice from 1789 to 1820, and every old sore was healed. Those members who had, during the pending difficulties, left the Church and united with other churches, returned home ere long, their sorrow turned into joy, and all could sing :

" Blest be the tie that binds
Our hearts in Christian love."

Nothing of marked interest occurred from this time until the close of the year 1836, when, after a long season of spiritual apathy, the Church was awakened to fervent and importunate prayer. The Lord heard, and in the years 1837-8 forty persons became the subjects of His saving grace. The effect of this revival on the benevolence of the Church was marked, its contributions being larger than ever before, while interest in all evangelical work both at home and abroad was greatly quickened.

In the year 1841 the Church united with thirteen others in New Jersey in organizing the East New Jersey Baptist Association, after a connection with the New York Association of forty-nine years.

After the subsidence of the revival of '37 there was no especial religious interest in the Church for several years, and only a few were added to the Church. But harmony and brotherly love prevailed and the prayers of pastor and people for yet larger displays of saving power and grace were unceasing. In the year 1843, God, in his great mercy, again visited the Church, and there was a great awakening. Nothing like it had hitherto been known in the Church's history. It pervaded the whole community and embraced all ages ; many that were heads of families and prominent citizens. The voice of weeping in tender contrition was heard on every side, followed by songs of thanksgiving in praise of the riches of redeeming grace. The pastor's hands and heart were full. Elders Webb and Hires came to his help and helped him much. His brethren, too, held up his hands, for all felt the power of the Spirit upon them. This work of grace continued for many weeks and even months, and within a year the number of souls added to the Church was one hundred and one. Brother George Drake, a licentiate of the Samptown Church, but recently united with this Church, rendered the pastor invaluable service throughout these meetings. He continued to preach the Gospel gratuitously wherever a door was opened, till his death in March, 1851. His name is held in grateful remembrance.

During this revival period many other churches in East Jersey enjoyed similar manifestations of God's presence. The church at New

Brunswick, of which the beloved and revered G. S. Webb was pastor, reported to the Association in the same year 37 baptized; Samptown, 115; First Plainfield, 62; Second Plainfield, 99; Rahway, 110; Middletown, 76; Northfield, 96. It was emphatically a year of blessing—of gathering in of sheaves.

The Lord prospered the ministry of Mr. Lewis and, through him, gathered into the fold one hundred and sixty-five souls. What was the character of these converts, and did they add real strength and lasting prosperity to the Church? Let us call the roll, only in part, and the question will be answered: Henry Smalley, Samuel Smith and Evalina, his wife; Henry Lupardus and Cornelia, his wife; Peter Smith, Noah Runyon, John Drake, Sarah Smith, Insley Boice, Runyon Walker, John Frantz, Reuben Drake, Augustus Stelle, Samuel C. Stelle, Isaac Stelle, David C. Dunn, Alexander Dunn, David Smith, William M. Drake, Richard Smith, Samuel R. Stelle, James D. Stelle, Jeremiah D. Stelle, Fitz Randolph Smith, Lewis F. Randolph, James T. Dunn, William F. Randolph, Peter A. Runyon, and many others, including honorable women not a few. Of those named here, seven or eight have served the Church as deacons—men who purchased to themselves a good degree and great boldness in the faith which is in Christ Jesus. As to the rest of these newly added members they have been burden-bearers and the bone and sinew of the Church. A few of them yet live. The greater part have crossed the stream and are now among the spirits of the just made perfect, and many there are here to-day to whom Heaven is all the dearer because *they* are there. The writer here ventures the opinion that rarely does a revival occur in any church that results in the addition of so many intelligent, stable and influential citizens, whose moulding influence on church and community is more after "a godly sort." To the praise of God's sovereign grace be it spoken and written.

Mr. Lewis continued to watch over these new-born souls with all fidelity, and over the whole flock of which the Lord had made him overseer, until the 25th of September, 1849, when he fell asleep in Jesus. His work was done, and well done.

> " Servant of God, well done ;
>   Rest from thy loved employ,
>   The battle fought, the victory won,
>   Enter thy Master's joy."

The Church, in grateful appreciation of his faithful service and Christian worth, met all his funeral expenses, erected a stone to his memory, and presented to his widow, the following Spring, $200. This lady was herself a beautiful specimen of Christian womanhood, and lived until August 17, 1876, when she passed away in full assurance of faith, having attained the ripe old age of nearly ninety-five years. Her remains were brought from Philadelphia and placed by those of her revered husband. Mr. and Mrs. Lewis had eleven children, of whom three died in early childhood. The eldest lived seventy-seven years, the youngest sixty-five. Two are still living, namely: Mrs. Caroline P., widow of Mr. William Farson, and Mrs. Charlotte Lee, widow of Franklin Lee, a deacon of the Second Baptist Church, Philadelphia, and for many years a member of the Corporation of the Philadelphia Association, and held in high esteem by that body. The memory of Mrs. Lee's active service, during the ministry of her father in this vineyard, no less than her many Christian virtues, lingers gratefully among her old friends in Piscataway. The excellent brother who briefly described Mr. McLaughlin speaks of Mr. Lewis as " a plain man who made no pretentions to either learning or eloquence, diffident and retiring in his manners, yet sound in the faith and earnest in his delivery of truth, seeking the honor of his Divine Master, and the peace and harmony of his people in which he was eminently successful; faithful in warning sinners of their danger and pointing out to them the way of salvation."

HENRY V. JONES, Eighth Pastor.
1850–1856.

After the death of Mr. Lewis, the Church, recognizing the need of divine guidance in the choice of a pastor, voted, November 28, 1849, " to hold a special meeting on the last Wednesday in every month for conference and prayer on the subject of obtaining a pastor, until the good Lord provide us one." These prayers were answered. Rev. H. V. Jones, of Newark, having been invited to visit the Church, accepted the invitation, and after preaching a week on the field he was unanimously called to the pastorate, January 30, 1850. This action of the Church was confirmed on the following Lord's day by the combined vote of the Church and congregation, and at a special meeting held February 5, it was voted that Mr. Jones should receive as salary $550 per annum in regular quarterly payments together with dwelling rent free, and the advantages of all the rents of the pews which might be received over and above the sum of $550.

Rev. Henry V. Jones was born in Welshpool, Montgomeryshire, North Wales, February 14, 1808, and left an orphan when four years old. He was baptized into the fellowship of the Dean Street Baptist Church, London, by the pastor, Rev. Benjamin Lewis, and was the next day disowned by his uncles with whom he had his home, and driven from their house for this act. He came to this country in 1831 ; commenced speaking in public while a member of the church in Lyons, N. Y., in 1834 ; was ordained at Williamson, N. Y., April 8, 1835, while supplying the church there. He became pastor successively of the churches at Palmyra, Milan, and Fabius, all in New York State, and in September, 1843, took charge of the First Baptist Church of Newark, N. J., where he remained till he came to Piscataway, April 1, 1850.

Mr. Jones' pastorate in Newark had been " eminently successful." Thus has it been characterized by Mr. Isaiah Peckham, writer of the history of that church, published in the Associational Minutes for 1876, and who proceeds to say :   " Mr. Jones baptized nearly one hundred, and received into the Church three times that number, leaving it at length harmonious and highly prosperous." The same writer, after speaking of that Church's growth and increased benevolence from year to year, gives honor to whom honor is due in the statement that "the secret of this advance was a more correct idea of the mission of a church. It was when this body, particularly under the ministry of Rev. H. V. Jones, in the colonizing of the South Church in February, 1850, really apprehended and began to act upon the Gospel idea of enlargement by activity, that it began to grow." These are words fitly spoken of a man, who, if he was not the actual father of the Newark Baptist City Mission, contributed more than any other man to its formation.   The germ of the plant was in his heart.

The ministry of Mr. Jones in this parish was greatly honored by the Lord, both in the winning of souls and in the up-building of the Church.   Full of the spirit of missions himself, the Church largely partook of the same, and responded heartily to all his propositions for securing systematic contributions to the various benevolent societies of our denomination.   Missionary societies had long existed in the Church, but as they had become more or less inefficient they were suspended, and, in stead, the parish was divided into seven districts with solicitors and collectors in each, with the design of awakening a yet greater interest in evangelical effort and securing something from every member towards sending the Gospel into all the world.

About a year before the close of Mr. Jones' pastorate, his health so greatly declined as to disqualify him for much of the labor incident to so large a field.   The Church, cherishing a warm appreciation of his ministry, granted him from time to time indefinite periods of rest, in the hope that he might recover his strength and for many years go in and out among them; but in this hope both he and they were disappointed, and in the month of March, 1856, he bade a tearful farewell to a deeply attached people. With respect to this event, he himself writes in a brief autobiographical paper : " I closed my labors with this beloved people after six years' service among them, during which period I received innumerable tokens of their affectionate esteem, and in no instance received from any person in the Church or congregation an unkind word or look ; but, broken down in health, and feeling utterly unfit to do the work in my opinion necessary in so large a field, I obtained a reluctant discharge to try the effect of sea air, and accepted the call of the Baptist Church in Noank, Ct., commencing my labors there, June 19, 1856." From Noank he removed to West Troy, April 1, 1864, to become pastor of the church there. In March, 1866, he returned to Noank, in answer to the earnest entreaty of that church which was now in so divided a condition as to require a man of his wisdom and prudence to bring order out of confusion. He remained there till December, 1869, when he accepted the pastorate of the Baptist Church in Princeton, N. J., trusting that his wife's health, now impaired, would be benefited by the change. In February, 1871, he accepted the position of Financial Secretary of the Board of Managers of the New Jersey Classical and Scientific Institute, at Hightstown. Having accomplished his assigned work, he gave up the books, and January 1, 1872, entered upon his duties as District Secretary of the American Baptist Home Mission Society for New Jersey and Delaware. In April, 1874, he engaged for a short time as Financial Agent of the Board of the South Jersey Institute. Then, to meet some exigency or special demand, he served the Institute yet another year. In every field he occupied as a pastor he served the Master according to the full measure of his strength, and in every trust committed to him was scrupulously faithful.

After leaving Princeton, Mr. Jones moved his family to New Bruns-wick. He was near the old parish, his visits to which and his occasional pulpit ministrations were sources of mutual enjoyment and profit. Mr. Jones was now approaching the age which the Psalmist defines as the ordinary limit of life. Indications of heart disease had presented them-selves some months before his death, giving him premonitions of a fatal issue sooner or later but occasioning no alarm to him, whose " life was hid with Christ in God." On a bright Summer morning in June, 1878, following a sermon in this pulpit, after spasms of intense pain, he closed his eyes on earth and all he loved most on earth, and opened them—who can doubt ?—in heaven.

Mr. Jones was a man of middle stature. He was endowed with a large share of common sense, and an amiable disposition. Naturally of much vivacity of spirits, sprightly in conversation, and warm-hearted, he was always a genial companion In the pulpit he was grave, often solemn, always plain and sensible, clear in his understanding of divine truth, and presenting it in all its simplicity, "warning every man and teaching every man in all wisdom that he might present every man perfect in Christ Jesus."

The remains of Mr. Jones were brought to the graveyard adjoining this house and laid by those of his devoted wife, who six years before had fallen asleep. There they await the resurrection of the just. The stone at the head of his grave, bearing evidence of its erection by filial love, has this inscription :

Our Father,

REV. HENRY V. JONES,

Died, June 17, 1878,

Aged, 70 years, 4 months and 3 days.

He kept the Faith.

CHRISTIAN J. PAGE, NINTH PASTOR.
1856–1867.

About five months after the close of Mr. Jones' ministry in this parish, a call was given to Rev. C. J. Page. Mr. Page was born in Baltimore, Md., December 25, 1822. In 1839 he united with the Second Baptist Church of Philadelphia, then under the pastoral care of Rev. Daniel Dodge. His literary studies were pursued in Philadelphia and at the Germantown Collegiate Institute. Mr. Dodge was his theological instructor. In March, 1846, he was ordained as pastor of the Union Baptist Church at Milestown, now one of the wards of Philadelphia, the ordaining council consisting of Rev. Richard Pickard, Rev. D. Dodge, Rev. Dr. G. S. Webb, Rev. G. I. Miles and Rev. George Higgins. After a pastorate of over five years, he removed to Bristol, Pa., where a church of only fourteen persons had been recently constituted, but without a house of worship. At the close of a ministry there of five and a half years he left a membership of one hundred and fifty, and in possession of a substantial and beautiful meeting-house, built of brown sandstone, which still stands and bears testimony to his interest and zeal in the Master's cause. He removed thence to this parish and began labors October 1, 1856. The Lord wrought with him effectually. A revival that attended protracted efforts at an out-station—the village of Piscatawaytown—resulted in numerous conversions, and within a period of about eighteen months, just one hundred persons were baptized and added to the Church. The total membership in 1858 reached two hundred and eighty-five, and in the following year two hundred and eighty-eight, a higher total than it had ever before attained.

As is usual after large ingatherings, a declension followed this season of refreshing, and in the five following years the additions by baptism were few. Besides, the political agitation of the country, followed by that terrible strife that absorbed the thoughts and sympathies of the people at large, were not favorable to the awakening of religious thought and feeling. At this time, or in the year 1862 when citizens everywhere were being drafted for the war, Piscataway township was about to be subjected to a draft for one hundred and ten men. Volunteers were in vain sought for. At a town meeting, held in this emergency, Mr. Page was not only requested but urged to take the command of a company, provided one could be formed. The company was formed, and true to his word, he went forth as its head to the conflict, the end of which no one could then foresee. When, however, it was found that he could better serve "the boys" as Chaplain, he was elected by the regiment,[1] with which the company was connected, to that position—a position much more consonant with his feelings and ministerial calling. At the same time the Church voted him leave of absence for nine months with the continuation of his salary.[2] Returning to his charge at the expiration of this time, the Head of the Church again smiled on the pastor's labors. In 1864 nearly forty persons were added to the Church by baptism, while each of the three following years witnessed many accessions. The whole number baptized by him during his pastorate was one hundred and fifty-five. The total membership at the close was two hundred and sixty-two.

In the month of March, 1867, Mr. Page tendered his resignation, and in the following Autumn removed to Spring Valley, N. Y., bearing with him the testimony of the Church that during the eleven years of his ministry among them he had been "abundant in labors, instant in season and out of season, earnest in contending for the faith, and faithful in seeking the peace, harmony and prosperity of the Church and the salvation of souls."

After leaving here, Mr. Page became successively the pastor of the Manuet Church, Rockland County, N. Y., two and one-half years; of

1. Twenty-eighth Regiment, New Jersey Volunteers.
2. The Church was ministered to during the pastor's absence by Rev. Dr. Webb.

the First Baptist Church, Peekskill, five and one-half years; of the Cold Spring Church, on the Hudson, seven years; of the First Church, Middletown, N. Y., where he still is, and has been the last seven years, and to it is devoting the ripe experience of a ministry of forty-three years and the sanctified energies of "a sound mind in a sound body."

JAMES F. BROWN, TENTH PASTOR.

1868–1878.

[Prepared by the present Pastor.]

The following sketch, found partly in the "Baptist Encyclopædia," is known to be an accurate outline of the prominent points in the history of Dr. Brown, prior to his settlement with the Piscataway Church.

James F. Brown, son of Rev. Thomas and Mary Brown, was born at Scotch Plains, N. J., July 4, 1819. He united with the Fifth Baptist Church, Philadelphia, in 1833, then under the care of Rev. Dr. J. L. Dagg; graduated from the University of Pennsylvania July, 1841; was licensed to preach by the First Baptist Church, Philadelphia, the same year; studied theology with Dr. Dagg, and was ordained in March, 1843, as pastor of the church at Gainsville, Ala.

In April, 1846, he became pastor of the Great Valley Baptist Church, Chester County, Pa., where his father had preceded him, remaining eight years, when he was called to Scotch Plains, his native place, in April, 1854, where also, long years before, his father had preceded him. After six years he accepted a call to the First Church, Bridgeton, N. J., June, 1860. From this position he was called to the Piscataway Church.

In 1863, the University at Lewisburg, Pa., conferred on him the Doctorate of Divinity. As a still more marked expression of the estimate in which he was held by his brethren, he was at one time elected to the Chancellorship of the University, and served in the relation of Chancellor several years.

During the pastorate of Dr. Brown, very important external changes took place in the Piscataway Church. The condition of the country and the spirit of the hour favored these movements. In the five years since the close of our civil war, the country had not only recovered from financial and other straits; there was a general rebound. Money, current in business, was abundant; real estate and every product brought into the market were at high prices—high beyond any precedent. Speculation was rife; and, among another class, was also awakened a wide-spread spirit of enterprise. The Lord gave unto pastor and people to see a

great opportunity: The parsonage, located a mile and a half distant
from the church edifice, with 20 acres of land attached to it, was disposed of, and in its place and with its avails one much more generous
and convenient on an eligible site near the church home was built.   An
oblong plot of one acre, barn and garden in the rear, and grounds tastefully laid out surrounding the dwelling, all provided for by the sale of
the other, was a long step forward.

The large, substantially built church edifice, occupying high ground,
was crowned with a graceful spire.   In a rural section as nowhere else,
and especially where an undulating landscape admits of a wide range of
the eye, and among a thoughtful people, such a spire is touchingly eloquent, and preaches perpetually to human hearts.   This one, seen from
a large number of homes in the different neighborhoods, is evermore
pointing hopefully from their sacred, central meeting place to Him who
is enthroned in the heavens.

A lecture room, needed for every department of church work, was
added on the rear of the main building, and at the same time was introduced a commodious baptistery, entered from the new lecture room.
These additions, though they had slept, were no more than the full com-
plement of the architect's original design, making the completed building impressively and gratefully symetrical.

In Piscatawaytown, two miles distant, where there is a larger and
closer settlement than in Stelton, a neat chapel of ample dimensions
was erected, with exclusive reference to the spiritual needs of that community.

These changes, external in their nature, eminently spiritual in their
influence, have become a kind of "fruit that remains."   Their influence,
quiet, untraceable and forevermore outreaching, will never be measured
or weighed till every secret thing is brought to light.   They make conspicuous to the eye, and will continue to do so everywhere about Stelton,
the hand of wise, far-sighted, Christian men under the moulding ministry of Dr. Brown.

And yet it was in the spiritual edification and building up of the
Church in order to stability, and for the wider ingathering of the lost
through the Church—it was in that line more especially that Dr. Brown
found the stimulus that never failed him, and the purest satisfaction ; and
under his administration the Church reached the greatest numerical
strength it has ever had.

All the benevolent enterprises of the denomination were fostered
by his ministry.   During his pastorate, under the inspiring lead of Mrs.

Brown, who was aided and encouraged in the undertaking by Miss M. A. Sutton, a sister whose earnest piety and life-long devotion to missionary and Sabbath School work gave her a wide influence among us—the "Judson Band" was organized as a missionary center in the Church, and further along sprang up the "Cheerful Workers," as also a missionary center, one composed of the elder and the other the younger sisters in the Church. The influence of these unpretentious but systematic and untiring workers has been, all along, as now, a continuous benediction.

As a preacher, Dr. Brown had few superiors. His ideal of preaching was so high that he could never reach it, and therefore he could see little occasion in his own preaching for self-gratulation. This modesty, always conspicuous, was inborn. But in the estimation of Dr. Greenleaf S. Webb, known so widely among Baptists and so long a father among New Jersey Baptists, Dr. Brown as a preacher, was second to no Baptist minister in the State. All through life he was a hard student, not sparing the midnight oil, and often forgetful of his bodily health, never robust. The strain at length proved too exacting. At the end of nine years, in 1877, his health had so far failed that he felt incompetent to meet the demands of this large field, and wished to resign. At the request of the Church a respite of some months was taken, but with no such results as encouraged him to look for a speedy return to work. His resignation was finally accepted in September, 1878.

The resolutions unanimously adopted at this time by the Church were so warm and full and overflowing, that we cannot refrain from introducing as much of them as space will permit.

There is first a full expression of deep sympathy with him in the common affliction. The following resolutions, after that, will clearly indicate the ground covered, and the place he held in the hearts of Church and people :

"RESOLVED, That during his ministry of ten years among us, our pastor enjoyed the fullest confidence of his brethren and the entire community, and has exerted an influence that will be long and powerfully felt for good by all who have enjoyed his wise and tender counsel, or witnessed his devoted Christian life.

"RESOLVED, That we bear our testimony to the untiring zeal with which, since he first entered upon his duties, he has labored in his Master's cause—his devotion to the spiritual interests of his people being so great that his growing bodily infirmities were either forgotten or ignored in his desire to serve them. His pulpit ministractions have always been full of comfort and edification to the Church ; and words cannot express our gratitude to God for the rich Biblical instruction we have received, and the steady growth in piety and knowledge that has been observable among us under his faithful ministrations. We desire, also, to testify to his ability and prudence as a safe leader and guide of God's people. The utmost harmony has prevailed during his entire ministry.

"RESOLVED, That though now formally parting as pastor and people, there can be no separation of the ties that unite our hearts in Christian love and fellowship. The work here performed can never be forgotten : and we feel assured that its fruits will appear through all the coming years to the praise and glory of our dear Redeemer's name.

After a rest of nearly seven years, preaching only occasionally, he took temporary charge of the church at Tunckhannock, Pa., in July, 1885. where he remained two and a half years, when finding himself unable to preach twice every Lord's day and to meet the other duties of his charge, he resigned the pastorate, but at the earnest request of the Church there continued to supply once each Lord's day for six months longer.

He has now felt obliged to retire altogether from active work in the ministry and has fixed his residence near that of his daughter's at Mullica Hill, Gloucester County, N. J., his general health impaired but his intellectual force not abated.

Though speaking of the living, it will hardly be considered indelicate, in closing this outline, to quote from a book so widely known as the "Baptist Encyclopædia," its own and comprehensive summary under this name : "A man of scholarly attainments, gentle spirit, sound theological views, large sympathies, and blessed in his ministry."

JOHN W. SARLES, ELEVENTH PASTOR.
1879.

Rev. John Wesley Sarles was born June 26, 1817, at Bedford, Westchester County, N. Y. He was born again, in New York city under the ministry of Dr. Spencer H. Cone, and was baptized by him April 5, 1835. By the same Church, the Oliver St. (now the Epiphany) he was licensed to preach in April, 1839. The same year he entered Madison University, and, after a full course of study in both the Literary and Theological Departments, graduated in August, 1847. In the month of October following, he was ordained in Brooklyn as pastor

of the Central Baptist Church, of which he was the first and only
pastor till March 31, 1879, a period of nearly thirty-two years.   On
the following day, April 1, he entered upon pastoral duties here to
which he had been unanimously invited the preceding February. This,
therefore, is his second charge.

Dr. Sarles' ministry here has been characterized by unwavering
fidelity to all pulpit and pastoral duties. From none of the latter,
although from the extent of the parish they have been necessarily
onerous, has he shrunk. His eyes have been on the whole field, and not
simply on the home field, but on " the field " which is " the world,"
his sympathies embracing evangelical work in all climes.   Hence his
care to foster the missionary spirit, and particularly among the young
people of the Church and congregation, and hence, too, the organization of two Societies, the " Light Bearers," at Stelton, and
the " Band of Hope," at Piscatawaytown, both which, in addition to
the " Judson Band " and the " Cheerful Workers," formed under the
preceding pastorate were intended to enlist the interest of the youngest
in the cause of missions.   The intent has been largely realized.

The " Society of Christian Endeavor," also recently organized,
is prosperous, and accomplishing good results, aiding especially the
younger members in conducting devotional meetings, contributing " to
the promotion of an earnest Christian life " among themselves, and to
greater zeal in the service of God.

In addition to the above Societies with their respective officers
there may be noted the organization by the ladies of a Temperance
Society, together with two little Bands for the children who are instructed in the subject, and induced to become total abstainers.

There have also been established monthly concerts of prayer, one
for missions, the other for Sunday-schools led by the superintendents.

Covenant meetings are held on Saturday preceding every com-
munion.   It will thus be seen that in respect to appliances for
Christian work, means for the development of gifts and graces of the
Spirit, for the encouragement of an active and aggressive piety and for
the recognition and acknowledgment of God as " all in all," nothing seems to be wanting.

Great care is also taken to carry out a firm but kind discipline in
the belief that the Lord of the Church cares for purity of life rather
than for swelling numbers of communicants who have only a name to

1. October 26, 1886.

live. In the desire to keep the Church pure, the members, happily, are of one mind with the pastor.

Justice would hardly be done to the honored pastor if no reference should be made to an evident characteristic of his inner Christian life, namely, his strong personal faith in God, in His word, in His special providential government of His Church and people, timing all changes and events, even the minutest circumstances of life in their interests, or for their present and eternal good. And it is the testimony of the members of this Church that the application of this faith to all the occurrences of life has been helpful to them and conducive to their abiding peace and happiness in God.

· The writer feels somewhat straitened in speaking more elaborately of this servant of God, particularly of his endowments both by nature and grace, and of his pulpit gifts, while he is yet living and in the pastorate. Some future historian will extol the grace that has made such prominent use of Dr. Sarles both in the Denomination at large and in the only two churches he has thus far served throughout a ministry of forty-two years.

MINISTERIAL GIFTS.

In the beginning of this sketch it was stated that three constituent members of the Church had been before its organization, recognized as exhorters, one of whom was ordained as its pastor. Whether they had been licensed before they came into the settlement, or, were afterwards informally requested by their brethren here to exhort and teach, does not appear. The latter alternative is more probable.

The third and fourth pastors, Isaac Stelle and Reune Runyon, were both born in the township, and licensed by the Church. With regard to Benjamin Stelle, the second pastor, there can be no other conclusion drawn than that he also received his license from this Church.

Benjamin Miller, the first pastor of the Scotch Plains Church, was born in Piscataway, it is said "about the year 1715." Of somewhat wayward tendencies in early life, he was awakened by a sermon preached by the celebrated Gilbert Tennent, then of New Brunswick, by whom he had been christened. A young man of talent and piety he was persuaded to enter upon a course of study preparatory to the ministry, but soon after doing so he was led by conviction to embrace Baptist views, whereupon he united with this Church. Previous reference to Mr. Miller in our narrative supersedes the necessity of further remark, save that after a pastorate of over thirty-four years at the Plains he died there, November 14, 1781, in the sixty-sixth year of his age.

More than a hundred years ago there was a certain member of the Church who, it was reported, "attempted to preach without the consent or knowledge of the Church." A special church meeting was called to "consider such conduct," and it appeared to the brethren, in solemn council assembled, that this brother had, "at some society meetings held in several neighborhoods proceeded too far by way of exhortation, which some call preaching, whereupon the Church proceeded to advise the brother to desist from such conduct, to which, as it was the voice of the Church, the brother cordially agreed. Nothing daunted, this brother, at the same meeting, "requested that he might be permitted to improve his gift, in order to make his usefulness as a preacher appear, upon which the Church concluded to take the matter into consideration until the next meeting of business."[1] At the next meeting, the Church again "expressed the opinion that it was best for him to give the matter up for the present." After a lapse of a year we find a record which shows that "the matter" had been given up only for the present. The request was renewed, and the Church, not wishing to take the sole responsibility of deciding so grave a matter, invited a number of members from neighboring sister churches to sit in council with a committee of this Church and give judgment in the case. The Council, "after duly considering every circumstance attending the affair, advised that it would, in their opinion, be most for the honor of the cause of religion that the brother give up any further thought of exercising in that way, to which he cordially agreed."[2]

In the month of June, 1791, Mr. Peter S. Bryant came before the Church with reference to licensure, and after a discourse by him, "the voice of the Church was unanimous that he should be encouraged to another opportunity." It does not appear from the minutes that this "other opportunity" ever presented itself, or that he was licensed by this Church at all. We know, however, that as a "licentiate of Piscataway" he was ordained as pastor of the Church at Lyons Farms, which relation he sustained for sixteen years. Mr. Bryant was scholarly, and withal an earnest worker in the vineyard. Outlines of two or three of his sermons fell into the writer's hands nearly forty years ago. Their penmanship is beautiful, the arrangement logical, the expression terse and clear, the subject matter evangelical. While at the Farms, Mr.

1. Old Minutes, p. 7.
2. Old Minutes, pp. 8, 13.

Bryant prepared an abridgement of Booth's work on Baptism, that it might obtain a more general circulation. Owing to ill health he retired from the active ministry and removed to Newark, where he died in 1808.

Henry Smalley, son of John Smalley, a worthy member of the Church, was born in Piscataway, October 23, 1765 ; graduated at Princeton College in 1786, soon after which he was licensed by the Church, and rendered valuable assistance to the aged pastor, Rev. Mr. Runyon. On November 8, 1790, he was ordained pastor of the First Cohansey Baptist Church, and there labored till his death, February 11, 1839, in the seventy-fourth year of his age, after a pastorate of nearly forty-nine years. Mr. Smalley was one of the excellent of the earth, and a wise master-builder. To his labors is to be attributed the formation of the Second Cohansey Church, now the First Baptist Church of Bridgeton, and the strengthening of the cause of our Lord throughout Cumberland County. It was the testimony of the late Judge L. Q. C. Elmer, of Bridgeton, that the great truths of the Gospel Mr. Smalley preached laid deep and broad foundations for an orderly and prosperous community. He commanded universal respect for his solid worth and blameless life ; and from his Church and Christians of every name, veneration and love for his work's sake. To the aged members of that parish who yet survive his ministry, his name is still as precious ointment.

Jacob Sutton was licensed in January, 1811. He preached for the Church at Penn's Neck, then recently formed, but after a brief ministry was called to his rest in 1814.

Lewis F. Stelle, son of Deacon Drake F. Stelle, united with the Church by baptism in 1840 ; was licensed to preach, September, 1843 ; ordained at Piscataway, May 28, 1846, having in the meantime pursued his studies at Hamilton Literary and Theological Institute. He was pastor successively of the churches at Herbertsville, Branchville and Bloomingdale. In all these places he was faithful in the Master's service. He died in 1863, aged forty-four years, leaving three young sons who early in life became God's children, and a widow who, only a few months since, died in faith, lamented by a large circle of friends.

> " None knew her but to love her,
> None named her but to praise."

In the month of April, 1844, Hezekiah Smith, a youth of eighteen years, son of Deacon Peter Smith, was encouraged, after trial of his gifts, to commence a course of preparatory study, He entered Hamilton with high hopes of future usefulness, but being suddenly arrested by disease he returned home and died in June of the same year.

Warren Randolph, D. D., was licensed May 26, 1847. He graduated at Brown University in 1851, and the same year was ordained as pastor of the High Street Baptist Church, Pawtucket, R. I. After remaining there one year he became pastor of the Eighth (now Jefferson) Street Church, Providence, R. I. Since this pastorate of five and a half years, he has been pastor successively of the First Church, Germantown, Pa.; of the Harvard Street Church, Boston ; of the Fifth Church, Philadelphia ; of the First Church, Indianapolis ; of the Central Church, Newport, R. I., where he now is, and has been for the last ten years. From January, 1877, to April, 1879, he was Sunday School Secretary of the American Baptist Publication Society. In 1872, at its formation, he was elected a member of the International Bible Lesson Committee, re-elected in 1878, and again in 1884, and has been Secretary of the committee from the beginning. Dr. Randolph has been so long and prominently before the denomination as to supersede the necessity of further remark.

Bergen Stelle, a brother of the above named Lewis F. Stelle, was licensed November 29, 1848. His first pastorate was at George's Road; his second and last at Cherryville. He died August 9 ,1864, in the forty-ninth year of his age, greatly beloved by all, particularly his brethren in the ministry.

Augustus Pawley was licensed March 24, 1860, but soon retired from the ministry.

Charles C. Smith was licensed October 2, 1860. He graduated in the collegiate and theological departments of Madison University; in the latter in 1869, and was ordained in March, 1870, as pastor of the Baptist Church at Cooperstown, N. Y. His next pastorate was that of the Hannibal Baptist Church, in Oswego County, N. Y. After remaining there about two years, he removed to Branford, Ct., and was pastor of the church in that place eight years. He is now pastor of the church at Hempstead, L. I. As a brother so well known and beloved by all, nothing more need be added.

HOUSES OF WORSHIP.

Mention has been made of the first " meetinge-house " built in Piscatawaytown. It does not appear from any documents now in exisence, or from traditions, that the Church made any attempt to build a house exclusively for worship and religious purposes, or any movement in that direction until April, 1731, when, with a wise forecast for the future—the settlements extending further back from the village every year—the Church bought a lot of 4 6-10 acres from Alexander Mc-Dowell, about a mile to the west of Piscatawaytown. This was eight years before the death of the first pastor. Not until 1748 did the time come to arise and build. In the tenth year of Rev. Benjamin Stelle's pastorate, a house 46x36 was erected on this lot. Morgan Edwards, who visited this parish during Mr. Runyon's ministry, and from him and old citizens gathered his data concerning the Church, speaks of this structure as a " well-finished house, but wanting the necessary convenience of a stove," from which statement it appears that for forty winters the congregation had worshipped without this "convenience," for, at a church meeting held May 30, 1798, " it was carried by vote that the Trustees devise means to procure a stove against next winter." In the month of October following, this "convenience" again came under grave consideration, and it was found that "such was the encouragement to proceed, that the Church requested the Trustees to procure it and what was necessary to put it up, and to fix a pulley to the door of the meeting-house." Let it go down to posterity that Brother Lewis Fitz Randolph had the honor of presenting this motion for the introduction of the first stove into the Piscataway meeting-house. The Clerk himself appears to have thought that the name should be embalmed in history, inasmuch as out of scores of resolutions passed by the Church during a long series of years, the name of no mover of any one of them appears save in the case of this stove. In climes farther towards the North pole than this, and in times later than 1798, the introduction of a stove into a meeting-house was regarded as a useless if not an impious innovation on established customs, and a reflection on the piety and dignity of the fathers and mothers of Israel of the olden times.

In the year 1785 a house for the sexton was ordered to be built on the meeting-house lot, 16x18. The minutes do not state whether it was really built. We find soon afterwards that the care of the meeting-house was assigned to different brethren from year to year. In May, 1793, the brother in charge declined to act any longer, the sum allowed for his services being deemed inadequate, whereupon, for the ensuing year, the person taking charge was "allowed forty shillings." Brother John F. Randolph acted as doorkeeper until 1798, when Deacon Pyatt was appointed, who was to have "two pounds, York money, for his services." His successor, the following year, was Brother John Dunham, at a salary of forty shillings. The next year Deacon Pyatt was appointed to "get some one to serve for $5." It may here be stated that the office of sexton from the earliest times until the present has been filled by brethren of the Church, some of whom have been the most prominent members of the Church and community, and that the salary has been for long years past largely in excess of " forty shillings."

The meeting-house built in 1748 stood until 1825, the sixth year of Mr. Dodge's ministry, when, on account of its insufficient size and age— it had withstood the storms of seventy-seven years—it was taken down and a new and more spacious one—a frame building modeled after that of the Plainfield Baptist meeting-house—but two feet longer—was erected on or near the same site, at a cost of about $3,000. Its size was 52x42 feet. On the 1st day of January, 1851, during Mr. Jones' pastorate, as the people were gathering for worship and business, this house took fire from a defect in the stovepipe, and burned to the ground. This was a grievous trial to the Church, not only because it involved outlays of money in addition to those that had already been incurred in building a parsonage, but because the house was dear to them by many tender associations, God having so often manifested himself to them therein in the sanctifying and saving power of his Spirit. Cast down but not destroyed, they at once resolved to rebuild, subscribed much of the money needed on the spot, and, within the same year (December 31) the present house, occupying the site of the former, was completed at a cost of about $7,000, and dedicated to the Lord. The sermon on the occasion was preached by Rev. Dr. Hague, then of Newark. While the Church was houseless it was invited by neighboring churches to hold services in their houses of worship. Such courtesies were extended by the Baptist Church in New Brunswick, the Samptown Church, the Seventh Day Baptist Church at New Market, and the Presbyterian Church at Metuchen, and were gratefully accepted and duly acknowledged.

The spire on this house was erected in 1870 according to the original design of the architect at a cost of $1,537. Its height is 130 feet from the ground and 94 feet from the top of the house. In the year 1874 the annex in the rear of the meeting-house was built—designed for robing rooms on baptismal occasions and for social meetings, the whole being so constructed as to be thrown into one room if occasion requires. About the same time an acoustic apparatus was placed in the church by private contributions.

The ladies of the Church in Piscatawaytown and vicinity, feeling the need of a chapel in that village for permanent religious worship and for Sunday-School purposes, took energetic measures towards erecting a

suitable building. Money was freely subscribed by members of the
Church and congregation in general, and in the summer of 1875 a tasteful and commodious house, known as the "chapel," was opened with
appropriate exercises, the dedicatory sermon being preached by Dr.
Warren Randolph, of Newport. The ground on which the chapel stands
was given by Mrs. Nancy Martin, a beloved sister of the Church. The
house cost about $2,500. A vigorous Sunday-School is maintained there
under the superintendency of Mr. William H. Stelle, and the pastor
statedly preaches there three Sunday evenings in each month of the
year. The deed for this property was conveyed to the Church in March,
1878.

Previous to the settlement of Mr. Jones, the Church, which hitherto
had owned no parsonage, took measures to provide a home for their
future pastors in the parish. A house and lot of 20 acres, adjoining
lands of Furman Stelle and Augustus Stelle, were bought, about two
miles from the meeting-house. The old house, in the process of remodel-
ing, gave way virtually to a new and more commodious one. The lot,
together with the new building, cost about $4,000. This house was occu-
pied by the pastors till 1869, when, owing to its distance from the meeting-house and the amount of land attached to it, which was deemed by
many an encumbrance rather than a benefit, it was sold at twice its
original cost, and a new and tasteful dwelling was erected on a lot of
one acre (bought of Deacon J. D. Stelle, for $600) within a few rods of the
meeting-house, at a cost of $7,700.

Sheds for horses and conveyances were built on the church lot in
the rear of the meeting-house by individual members of the Church and
congregation in the year 1872.

The cost of the chapel, the spire, the baptistery, all accomplished
between 1869 and 1876, was about $7,000. This period was one of
marked progress in all the temporal and material interests of the Church,
and not without tokens of the presence of the quickening Spirit.

FAITH, DISCIPLINE AND GOVERNMENT.

We do not know what Confession of Faith, if any, was adopted by
the Church at the time of its organization. The probability is that it
adopted some form of "creed-statement," our denomination having
been among the earliest, if not "the earliest of the dissenting bodies
of England in the issuing of Confessions."[1] From the time of its con-

1. See Cuttings Vindication, p. 85.

nection with the Philadelphia Association in 1707, the Confession then or soon afterwards adopted by that body, and known as the Philadelphia Confession of Faith, was generally adopted by the churches in the provinces now known as the Middle States and by some in New England. This Confession was a reprint of " The Confession of Faith put forth by the Elders and Brethren of many congregations of Christians (baptized upon profession of their faith) in London and the country, A. D. 1689," the very year that this Church was constituted. This Confession having been "owned" by the Association, there can scarcely be a question that it was "owned" by this Church.

In the time of Mr. Dodge's ministry a Confession prepared by him was adopted by the Church. Briefer than that of the Philadelphia Confession, it contained the substance of its fundamental Articles. This Confession was still further abridged in the year 1836, during the pastorate of Mr. Lewis, but just how far we are left only to conjecture as it does not appear in the minutes. We may naturally infer that it was purged of all articles requiring the imposition of hands after baptism, and of all prohibitions of marriages within the fourth degree of consanguinity. In the year 1854, at the suggestion of Brother Augustus Stelle, a Committee was appointed to revise and amend this Confession, or report one "more satisfactory in some points." The committee, consisting of the pastor, Mr. Jones, and deacons Henry Smalley and Alexander Dunn, together with Brethren Samuel Smith and Augustus Stelle, reported in September, 1854, that they had "agreed to present for the adoption of the Church the Articles of Faith as adopted by the South Baptist Church of Newark, being in doctrine the same as our old Articles, only differing mainly in manner of expression, and proved by numerous quotations from scripture." These articles together with a Church Covenant were "adopted unanimously as expressive of our views of Gospel Truth and Christian fellowship" at a stated meeting of the Church, held March 24, 1855. They are the same in substance as those of the New Hampshire Confession. Hence the orthodoxy of the Church and its claim to abide in the faith of their fathers and of the Apostles and Prophets cannot be held in question. The Articles and Covenant are written in pages 1 to 5 of the New Book of Minutes, and are styled ARTICLES OF FAITH AND A CHURCH COVENANT OF THE FIRST BAPTIST CHURCH OF PISCATAWAY.

It is in place, therefore, here to state that while the corporate name of this Church was from 1781, and probably from its origin,

"The First Day Baptist Society" of Piscataway, it was, in the year 1874, under a general act of the Legislature appertaining to the incorporation of Trustees of Religious Societies, so changed as to read and be known henceforth as the FIRST BAPTIST CHURCH OF PISCATAWAY.[1]

A few words with regard to discipline may suffice. The Church, holding in common with Baptist churches the world over that none but a regenerate people has a scriptural right to the two ordinances of the New Testament, has, from the beginning, been careful to admit no others to membership. The utmost care, however, does not always avail to keep out either the self-deceived or deceivers, nor render any untemptible by the world, the flesh and the devil. When members have been found walking disorderly, or not according to the Gospel, they have been kindly admonished, reproved, rebuked, and if they still remain incorrigible, they have been put away as unworthy of a place in a Gospel Church. Intemperance and every other vice, and every species of immorality has incurred the highest penalty a church can inflict—exclusion. But with firmness in maintaining discipline, there have been united the utmost forbearance and tenderness, and sometimes a long suffering almost without a parallel. The early records reveal a case of discipline that was before the Church for six years and eight months before a decision was reached ; so scrupulous was it lest the least injustice should be done to the offending member. Indifference to the means of grace as manifested in forsaking the assembly of the saints or in withholding for the support of the Gospel, has never been winked at, or regarded as a trivial offence. On the contrary persistence in this wrong, in despite of all kindly efforts to induce a return to the fold, has been followed by exclusion. By rule, members who remove to the vicinity of other churches are required to remove also their membership to such churches unless peculiar circumstances make it inexpedient for them to do so. But the mere plea of attachment to the dear old mother, the Church of their first love, is not deemed an adequate excuse for remaining in her bosom.

CHURCH PSALMODY.

At the period of Baptist history when this Church was constituted, the propriety of singing in public assemblies was in much dispute. In England the celebrated Benjamin Keach, a contemporary of Bunyan,

---

1. While this is, geographically, a misnomer, the House of Worship being now in Raritan Township, the corporate title is not thereby affected.

and Kiffin and Hanserd Knollys, 1640–1704, had great difficulty we are told, in introducing the practice of singing in the Church under his care. He wrote a book in defence of his views, entitled "*The Breach Repaired in God's Worship, or Singing of Psalms, Hymns and Spiritual Songs, proved to be a Holy Ordinance of Jesus Christ.*" This work brought on him much trouble and ill-will. For years some of his brethren opposed the practice, and finally seceded and founded a church upon the same principles, *singing only excepted.*[1] In this country the Second Baptist Church at Newport was founded in 1656, by twenty-one persons who seceded from the First Church on account of the use of Psalmody to which they objected, and to some other points, one of which was the indifference of the First Church to the laying on of hands at the admission of members.[2] At Cohansey, singing psalms met with opposition. Morgan Edwards thinks that "the Welch Tract Church, founded in 1707, was the principle, if not the sole means of introducing singing, imposition of hands and church covenants among the Baptists of the Middle States.[3] If Edwards' opinion be correct we must not conceive of the constituent members of this Church as singing psalms and hymns in their religious assemblies, but as refraining from making melody, except in heart, to the Lord. At what precise time the practice of singing was introduced, the recovery of the lost minutes could alone enable as to determine.

The first minute in regard to singing on the existing records reads thus: March 27, 1793: "Brother Oliver Stelle appointed a Clerk for the Society to raise the tunes in public worship, and Bro. Hezekiah Smith to supply occasionally." Under June 25, 1794, we find that Bro. Hezekiah Smith was promoted to the place of chief chorister and "the second appointment was taken under consideration until our next meeting of business." As the years roll on the number of assistant singers is increased. Thus, under date of May 24, 1826, we find it "ordered that Peter Smith, Samuel Smith, James Martin and James Dunham be invited to assist Bro. Thomas Randolph in singing." In 1832 there must have been a famous choir though not so designated ; the following persons "being requested and appointed to assist in singing: Robert Walker, Samuel Smith, Peter Smith, Justus Runyon, Runyon Walker, Stelle Runyon, Abel S. Runyon, Drake Stelle Samuel Stelle, James Dunham, Daniel Runyon, Isaac A. Stelle, Isaac Stelle

1. See Cramp's History, &c., pp. 387, 388.
2. Cramp, p. 463.
3. Morgan Edward's Materials. (Del.) pp. 232, 233.

Jr., and Joseph Sutton," fourteen male voices! The music was congregational, and of course the beautiful voices of the sisterhood chimed in with those of their brothers, all in harmony swelling. We can only imagine how the music of that time must have sounded and resounded within and around the courts of the Lord's House. If, perchance, that of the present time is more artistic, will any be bold enough to say it is more fervent, more devotional, or more in harmony with the spirit of true praise?

The minutes have been searched in vain to find out the hymn book that was used a hundred or even seventy-five years ago. Nor do any who are now living seem to remember what book was used as late as the time of Mr. Dodge. Most likely it was Parkinson's collection, or possibly, that of Dr. Watts. Soon after this period "Watts and Rippon" was introduced, and continued in use until 1872, when, there being no more copies to be had, the Baptist Hymn and Tune Book was adopted, and is still in use.

A choir was organized, probably not more than forty or forty-five years ago. But the leader has always been appointed by the Church. The first instrument of music, a cabinet organ, was introduced in 1866. This and its successors have just given place to the pipe organ, the sweet tones of which have fallen on our ears to-day.[1] Thus the church, abreast with the spirit of the age, enters upon its third century of existence by praising God, like holy men of the olden time of Israels' greatness with sound of voice and organ. Ps. 150 : 4.

BENEVOLENCE.

Reference has been already made to the interest of the Church in missions. Missionary societies were formed as early as Mr. Dodge's time, and from thence onward to the present time the Church has been in sympathy with the evangelical and educational enterprises of the age. Institutions of learning, temperance societies, missionary and Bible societies, feeble churches, the State Mission and Education societies, receive yearly contributions. In addition to collections in the church and congregation at stated times through the year for these various objects, there are, and have been for years past, three missionary societies, viz : The Judson Band, the Cheerful Workers and Light Bearers. The first or Judson Band, is composed of ladies of the Church

1. This instrument, with the alterations in the house required for its erection, cost about $2,600 - including cost of refurnishing about $500.

and congregation, the second of the young people—organized by that faithful worker in the Church, Miss Anna F. R. Smith—the third of the juvenile members of the congregation, mostly connected with the Sunday-Schools. These three societies collect on an average over $300 per annum for mission purposes. Another missionary society called Band of Hope, was formed in 1887 and has raised $30 per year. In the Sunday-Schools collections are taken at every session for some evangelical object, the specific object being designated at the end of every quarter. The young people are thus being trained to benevolence.

The table that follows will show the amounts that have been contributed for missions, education, and sundry objects for the last ten years by the Church, the societies and Sunday-Schools :

	1879	1880	1881	1882	1883	1884	1885	1886	1887	1888
A. B. M. Union..........	$84 00	$157 06	$118 44	$147 42	$104 50	$182 76	$197 58	$159 82	$146 86	$165 46
A. B. H. M. Society..........	54 39	105 87	122 28	290 00	198 85	230 46	247 26	199 97	192 57	201 96
A. B. Pub. Society..........	56 70	76 00	101 57	64 68	110 55	116 22	95 38	85 96	74 14	177 00
Bible Cause..............	25 20			30 00		165 32	87 42			
N. J. State Convention......	50 51	110 00	110 00	256 00	163 00	169 00	199 75	168 17	128 00	145 00
N. J. Education Society..	46 00	57 85	43 00	61 62	71 85	72 00	64 21	63 80	60 00	56 25
Feeble Churches			59 08	38 00	11 00					
Sundries..	382 03		258 39	522 00		215 55	116 00	139 31	271 43	280 85
Women's Foreign Mission,	200 00	200 25	211 83	290 00	250 00	255 00	235 00	291 00	265 50	280 49
" Home Mission...		30 25	75 00	90 00	139 00	106 00	56 63	103 56	142 00	283 80
Total for each year......	$841 83	723 25	1,089 21	1,666 12	1,028 73	1,503 31	1,399 22	1,203 30	1,280 20	1,540 81

Total for ten years, $12,176.40

From this table it appears that the contributions of the Church for the last ten years for Foreign Missions, have been $1,393.90
Of the Societies for the same object,   2,372.07

Making a total of $3,765.97

Contributions during the same period for Home Missions:

By Church, $1,843.31
By Societies,   958.24

Total, $2,801.55

Contributions of Sunday-Schools during the last eight years for Home and Foreign Missions, N. J. State Convention, Education Society, Publication Society, Bible work and Miscellaneous objects, $1,263.21

In addition to the several societies of a missionary character, before named, there is also a Young People's Society of Christian Endeavor, the object of which is to promote an earnest Christian life among its members; to increase their mutual acquaintance, and to make them more useful in the service of God. The Society was organized October 26, 1887.

MISCELLANEOUS MATTERS.

Reference has been made to the grave-yard at Piscatawaytown in which lie the remains of the early pastors and many other members of the Church and congregation. By a deed of the Lord Proprietors in 1695 (now on record among colonial documents at Perth Amboy), a large tract of land was conveyed by them to the township for a burial place and a training ground for the militia. No other objects are specified. The boundaries are clearly defined in the deed. The ground now fenced in as a grave-yard, together with the adjacent common, is but a small part of the tract bounded and defined by the deed. An Episcopal meeting-house stands in the enclosed part, another building, a school-house, stands on the commons just outside the enclosure. When and by whom the other part of this tract of land defined by the deed was, in the course of time, gradually encroached upon, to the perversion of the purpose set forth by the Lord Proprietors in this noted instrument, let those who are curious inquire.

The first Sunday-School established in the parish was begun at Piscatawaytown about the year 1820 or 1821. To Miss Ann Eliza Arnold (afterwards Mrs. Peter Tenbrook) belongs the honor of having originated this school. During the first summer it was held in a basement room of her mother's house. In the second summer so large was the attendance that it became necessary to resort to the school-house, where, after the lapse of a few years, Judge Cook, of New Brunswick, became its superintendent. The school is maintained to this day, its home now being the chapel. Its present superintendent is Mr. William H. Stelle. Besides this school there are four others.

2. The one at Stelton, held in the lecture room; Superintendent Deacon Peter R. Letson. Of all the schools this is the most recent, having been established in May, 1877.

3. The one at Friendship School-House; Superintendent, Benjamin S. Letson. Established 1834.

4. The one at New Durham ; Superintendent Deacon Wm. Dunn. Established 1835.

5. The one at Union School-house ; Superintendent Lewis Walker. Established 1835.

The last four schools were until a few years ago closed during the winter months. They are now open all the year. The International Lessons are used in all of them. In all of them many have been born into the kingdom.

As early as 1807 we find mention made in the Trustee Book of a lot, known as the Church Lot, adjoining or near the present meeting-house. This was rented for a long series of years to different persons for an amount varying from seven to fifteen dollars, until March, 1850, when it was sold to Isaac A. Stelle for $62 50-100 per acre.

In April of the same year ten acres of the parsonage farm were sold to Augustus T. Stelle for $365.00, thus reducing the original size of the farm which was thirty acres to twenty acres. This farm was bought of a Mr. Buchanan.

In the Minutes of the Trustees under date of January 18, 1804, we find this resolution, which explains itself: "Resolved, That traveling ministers who preach for the congregation at the meeting-house by appointment, shall be entitled to two dollars, and those who preach at private houses by appointment, transmitted by said minister and published by the pastor of the Church or some one of the Society, shall be entitled to one dollar out of the collections, or any other money belonging to the Society." Small as this amount was singly it amounted in the aggregate to a good round sum. We find the Treasurer crediting himself this same year : "By payment to several ministers, £2 ; in 1806, £1 4s. ; in 1807, " by cash paid sundry elders, £4 ; in 1809, $11 ; in 1812, $50.50, etc. This resolution was, in the course of time, so amended as, that nothing was to be paid to those who preached at private houses, and no doubt wisely amended. Unquestionably the Piscataway parish was not shunned by traveling ministers, as the records show. This custom lasted till 1849, this being the last date of payment made to such ministers.

The annual expenses of the Church were up to 1882 met by assessments on the pews. Since that time, by the envelope system, or weekly offerings of the members. This plan has been successful beyond the anticipations of its projectors, a larger amount being raised than by the former method, while it is believed to be more in accordance with the Covenant obligations of each and every member.

Last but not least of these miscellaneous items, we would tenderly record the fact that in the adjoining graveyard stands a marble shaft, erected by voluntary subscriptions, in grateful and loving memory of those members of the Church and congregation who fell in defence of their country in the late civil war, and belonging to Co. C., 28th Regiment, N. J., Volunteers. Let their names be recorded here.

MEMBERS OF THE CHURCH.

DAVID S. SMITH,
HENRY BRANTINGHAM,
GEORGE D. BOICE.

MEMBERS OF THE CONGREGATION.

PETER F. RUNYON,
JOEL F. LANGSTAFF,
MARTIN V. B. McCRAY,
WILLIAM M. MERRIL,
JEREMIAH R. FIELD,
CHARLES W. TOUPET,
CLARENCE D. GREEN,
AARON H. LANE,
SAMUEL BAKER.

RETROSPECT.

Having thus briefly traced the history of the Church—how imperfectly none can be more conscious than the writer—it remains only to take a brief retrospect and indulge in one or two reflections.

We have seen that the Church, during its two centuries of existence has had eleven, rather *has had* ten pastors, the eleventh being still in charge. Of these the longest pastorate, the first, was fifty years, the shortest five years. The first four and the seventh died on the field, full of years and honors, all loved and lamented by the Church. Of the remaining five who left the field to labor elsewhere, two only survive, one of whom has recently retired from pastoral work.

The total membership in 1800 was one hundred and twenty-four. Since then seven hundred and forty have been added by baptism.

What the membership has been every year since 1762, may be learned from the tabular statement appended. The largest number of baptisms in any decade was one hundred and fifty-six, viz.: 1850–1860. The total membership at the present time is two hundred and thirty. It reached its highest total in 1876, namely : three hundred and five. But numbers are not always an index of prosperity. In brotherly love and unity of spirit, in real activity, in well directed and prayerful effort for the spread of the Gospel at home and abroad, and in consecration of means to this end, the Church is to-day in no respect behind, but rather in advance of any former period.

Within the last century twenty-seven good men and true have by the choice of the Church served it as deacons. The early records refer frequently to Edward Griffith as one called to preside at meetings of business and to act on important committees. He was evidently held in high esteem as a man of intelligence and Christian worth. His grave stone, which almost touches this building, tells us that " he worthily fulfilled the office of deacon nearly fifty years." Time and lack of information forbid us to attempt to do justice to the memory of the greater part of those who have served in the same capacity since his day. But in respect to those who honored this office during, or just before the time of the writer, such as Jeremiah D. Stelle, David C. Dunn, Peter Smith, Alexander Dunn, Samuel Smith, Henry Smalley, Augustus T. Stelle, Furman Stelle, James D. Stelle, all of whom except the last named[1] are at home with the Lord. Was ever a church favored with better deacons, or pastor with men wiser in council, sounder in judgment, truer in friendship, more exemplary in Christian virtues? Why add more ? Their record is on high. In loving memory of their worth and work these words drop from our pen.

Whether we contemplate God's goodness to this Church in the generations past or in the times that now are, the feeling of gratitude must spontaneously rise up in every heart. If it has passed through some trials and sorrows, if there have been times of declension and a withdrawal of the quickening power of the spirit, its experience in these respects has not been peculiar, God dealing with churches as with individual members, bringing the trial, the sorrow and the cloud to chasten them that they may be driven closer to the throne of grace, take firmer hold of the promises, and more thoroughly realize that their sufficiency is of Him, of Him only.

Many churches in the old agricultural districts of our country

---

1. Now a member of Dr. Judson's Church, New York.

have, within the last fifty years, dwindled away, while many others maintain but a feeble existence. This Church is yet strong and bringing forth fruit in its old age. The territory acquired by the fathers, the sons through successive generations have stepped into, and entered into their labors. The Drakes and Runyons, and Dunns and Dunhams, and Randolphs and Stelles are here to-day, responding, in the fulness of their hearts, to the words of the Psalmist—"Thy faithfulness is unto all generations." Seldom in the history of churches has any church held the ground so long intact without occupancy by churches of other denominations. The Lord of the vineyard appears to have given it to this people, we trust, *in perpetuum*—forever. It is a goodly heritage and precious in its memories; but safe, only as those who now occupy it and those who follow them shall abide in the faith of the Gospel and have power with God in prayer. Their ancestry, those who gave tone to society and laid sure foundations for an orderly and prosperous community were men that feared God and wrought righteousness. And largely because of their piety and fidelity to truth is it that this community through all its history has been so abundantly favored temporally and spiritually. Piety, it is true, is not transmitted by birth, but waits upon and intercedes with the prayer-hearing God, and He is pleased to bless the children for their parents' sake. Who will attempt to measure the blessings that have fallen on this generation, in answer to the prayers of those who lived and toiled and wept in time long past? Their tears are bottled in Heaven. Their prayers and tears, added to those of their children, must ever come into remembrance before Him who is "the faithful God, who keepeth covenant and mercy with them that love Him and keep His commandments to a thousand generations," and they shall be the people whose God is the Lord, realizing all that the Psalmist longed for and prayed for : "Peace be within thy walls, and prosperity within thy palaces. For my brethren and companions sake I will now say, Peace be within thee."

THE STATISTICAL CONDITION OF THE CHURCH,

From 1762–1889.

The following table is compiled from the Minutes of the Phila-delphia, New York and East New Jersey Associations.   The first tabu-lated statement of the condition of the churches in the Century Minutes of the Philadelphia Association is found in the Minutes of 1761.   But the Church at Piscataway seems to have furnished no statistics that year. The table, therefore, begins with A. D. 1762 :

The want of agreement in the sum total in membership of one year with another, in the following table, is due to errors in the Minutes from which it was copied.

Year.	MINISTER	Where Held.	Baptized.	Rec'd by Letter.	Restored.	Dismissed.	Excluded.	Died.	Members.
1762	Isaac Stelle,		1	....	..	....		1	41
1763	"		2	....	..	....		....	43
1764	"		17	....	..	1		1	58
1765	"		4	..	..	..		2	60
1766	"		3	...	....	..		..	63
1767	"			...	....			.	63
1768	"		4	..	....	...		2	14
1769	"		7	....	. .	..		2	69
1770	"		8	....	...			2	73
1771	"		1	....	..	..		1	72
1772	"		1	....	..	....			73
1773	"		2	1	....	2		2	72
1774	"			...	..	....			72
1775	"		3	..	..	....	..	..	75
1776	"	Scotch Plains,	2	....	..	..		2	75
1777	"	{ No Ass'n this year, Phila. occupied by British army.		....					....
1778	"	{ No statistics in the Minutes.	....	..		..			
1779	"	" "				....		....	....
1780	"	" "	..		..			....	...
1781	{ No messengers nor letter sent.				....				
1782	(Without a pastor).	(No statistics).			..			....	1
1783	"	(Not represented.)		..		....	..	.	.
1784	Reune Runyon,	Ass'n, New York.	2				....	2	40
1785	"		..			.	1	...	39
1786	"		78	3	..				121
1787	"		22	....		1		2	140
1788	"		8	....	2			1	145
1789	"		4	2	2			2	147
1790	"	Ass'n, New York.	1	1	..			1	148
1791	"		1	1	....	4	2	3	141
1792	"	Ass'n, New York.	.		3	1		3	136
1793	"				2	....		1	133
1794	"				....		....		
1795	"		..	1	....	....	..		
1796	"				....		....		

Year.	MINISTER.	Where Held.	Baptized.	Rec'd by Letter.	Restored.	Dismissed.	Excluded.	Died.	Members.
1797	Reune Runyon,		...	...	1	1	...	1	118
1799	"		1	1		1	...	2	126
1800	"		6	1	....	3	3	2	124
1801	"		...	...	...	...		...	124
1802	"		...	2	..	1	...	2	123
1803	"		...	..	.	....	..	..	123
1804	"		..			...	.	.	....
1805	"		..				..	....	
1806	"		...		....	3	..	7	113
1807	"					.	....		
1808	"		14	...	..	4	.	...	123
1809	"		22	...	..	...	....	2	140
1810	"		2	2		...	....		144
1811	"		8				....	3	149
1812	James McLaughlin,		4	1	..		2	4	145
1813	"					....	....		.....
1814	"		..			...	....		
1815	"		4	..		...		4	142
1816	"	New Brunswick,	4	..	..				143
1817	"		5	....	....	26*	....	..	122
1818	Daniel Dodge,		....		....	5		3	113
1819	"		30	2	..	3	..	1	115
1820	"	Piscataway,	19			3	..	2	129
1821	"		7	2	2	..		2	134
1822	"	Plainfield,	1		...	1	..	4	130
1823	"		3	....				4	125
1824	"	Middletown,	3		.	....	..	3	135
1825	"		3	1	.	..	....	4	139
1826	"		1		....	1	...	10	129
1827	"		15	..	....	2	1	2	139
1828	"	Piscataway,	2			...	1	6	134
1829	"		1	..		2	....	2	131
1830	"	Newark,	1	..	....	5	1	5	120
1831	"		1		.	1	1	5	114
1832	"	Scotch Plains,	18	2	1	4	1	....	129
1833			.		...	4		....	125
1834	Daniel D. Lewis,	Samptown,	...	2		5	1	2	116
1835	"		1	2		5	....	3	111
1836	"	Paterson,	4	3	.		1	2	111
1837	"		18	1	..	11	1	4	115
1838	"	New Brunswick,	27	5	....	3	1	3	140
1839	"		4		....	2	....	1	141
1840	"	Middletown,		2	....	.	....	2	141
1841	"		1	1		..	....	3	143
1842	"	E. N.J. Ass'n, Pl'fie'd,	1	3	..	2	....	3	140
1843	"	First Church, Newark,	90	1	....	3	2	3	223
1844	"	Second, Middletown,	11	2	2	7	1	1	229
1845	"	Samptown,		1	1	3	2	3	223
1846	"	Patterson,		1	....		2	2	219
1847	"	New Brunswick,	...			4	1	5	209
1848	"	Second, Plainfield,	1	2	....	2	2	2	204
1849	"	Rahway,	..	1		3	1	6	194

* Twenty-three of these were dismissed from the Church in New Brunswick

Year.	MINISTER.	Where Held.	Baptized.	Rec'd by Letter.	Restored.	Dismissed.	Excluded.	Died.	Members.
1850	H. V. Jones,	Middletown,	....	..	...	4		4	189
1851	"	Newark,	24	4	...	3	...	7	207
1852	"	Piscataway,	3	....	....	5	....	7	194
1853	"	Scotch Plains,	13	2	....	11	1	3	198
1854	"	Hoboken,	10	5	1	2	...	2	211
1855	"	Holmdel,	3	8	....	4	...	3	209
1856		Bloomfield,	8	1	..	2	1	2	214
1857	C. J. Page,	Shrewsbury,	46	8	..	6	....	5	254
1858	"	Plainfield,	44	2		4	1	5	285
1859	"	Morristown,	5	2	2	4	2	1	288
1860	"	Jersey City,	3	3	....	8	3	4	282
1861	"	Middletown,	2	2	....	3	2	5	277
1862	"	Piscataway,	..	1	....	3		3	273
1863	"	North, Orange,		....	2	..	9	262	
1864	"	Red Bank,	38	...		7	..	8	282
1865	"	South Newark,	4	4	....	3	1	4	282
1866	"	Paterson,	13	2	....	6	1	3	285
1867	"	New Monmouth,	3	....		5	7	1	262
1868	James F. Brown,	Rahway,	8	3	...	11	2	3	268
1869	"	North, Jersey City,	4	2	..	3	8	2	261
1870	"	Amboy,	8	1	..	8	2	3	255
1871	"	Plainfield,	23	5	..	2	1	2	276
1872	"	First. Elizabeth,	2	1		4	1	6	268
1873	"	Bergen,	..		....	2	....	4	276
1874	"	Scotch Plains,	7	2	...	1		2	262
1875	"	Red Bank,	21	1	...	1	6	5	292
1876	"	New Market,	15	3		5	...	3	305
1877	"	Piscataway,	1	1	....	5	1	4	299
1878	"	South, Newark,	...	3		7		7	288
1879	J. W. Sarles,	Red Bank,	3	8	....	11	3	5	279
1880	"	First, Plainfield,	7	..	....	4	....	5	277
1881	"	First, Newark,	26	3	...	8	...	8	292
1882	"	North, Jersey City,		1	...	6	1	9	276
1883	"	Rahway,	11	.		...	1	5	271
1884	"	South, Newark,	7	4		4	1	8	269
1885	"	Red Bank,	10	...	....	4	8	8	265
1886	"	New Market,	8	1	2	4	1	8	263
1887	"	Piscataway,	8	1	1	7	5	7	249
1888	"	Fairmount, Newark,	6	3	..	16	9	2	231
1889	"	Park Ave., Plainfield,	4	1	....	4	3	4	225

OFFICERS OF THE CHURCH.

John W. Sarles, D. D., Pastor.

Deacons.	Trustees.
Wm. Crowell,	Bergen D. Stelle,
Peter R. Letson,	Frank Davis,
Mefford Runyon,	Noah D. Runyon,
William P. Dunn,	Wm M. Letson,
Samuel E. Stelle,	Benj. S. Letson,
Warren Smalley.	Mefford Runyon,
	Isaac Dayton.

B. D. Stelle. *Chairman.*

Wm. M. Letson, *Secretary.*

Church Clerk.
Peter A. Runyon.

Church Treasurer,
Peter R. Letson.

Sexton.
Theodore Mundy.

Sexton of Chapel.
Mahlon Mundy.

Deacons of the Church from 1781 to the present time. When elected, and time of service.

	APPOINTED.	DIED.
Edward Griffith,		March 24, 1813.
Asa Runyon,	October, 1789,	No record.
Benjamin Stelle,	"	
Ephraim Pyatt,	August, 1792,	August 10, 1813.
Joseph Holton,	October 31, 1804,	February, 1805.
George Drake,	August 28, 1805,	
Peter Runyon. Jr.,	November 3, 1813,	April 13, 1834.
Hezekiah Smith	" "	November 2, 1817.
John F. Randolph,	November 26, 1817,	April 6, 1826.
Wm. F. Manning,	June 2, 1821,	July, 1850.
Isaac A. Stelle,	May 24, 1826,	June 3, 1872.
Drake Stelle,	February 27, 1833,	February 11, 1855.
Peter Smith,	August 28, 1839,	February 2, 1853.
Henry Smalley,	" "	December 11, 1854.
Jeremiah D Stelle,	March 3, 1852,	April, 1857.
Alexander Dunn,	" "	April 20, 1875.
David C. Dunn,	" "	June, 1856.
Samuel Smith,	September 29, 1855,	August 2, 1881.
Augustus T. Stelle,	" "	September 20, 1887.
Jas. D. Stelle,	" "	Membership transf'd
Peter R. Letson,	July 27, 1872,	
Wm. Crowell,	" "	
Furman Stelle,	" "	December 28, 1880
Mefford Runyon,	November 29, 1879,	
Wm. P. Dunn,	" "	
Warren Smalley,	November 28, 1885,	
Samuel E. Stelle,	" "	

Stated Clerks from 1793 to the present time.

NAMES.	WHEN APPOINTED
Louis Dunn,	April, 1793.
George Drake,	October, 1796.
William F. Manning,	May 1820.
Samuel Smith,	November, 1837.
Joseph H. Smith,	September, 1855.
Lewis F. Stelle,	March, 1862.
Augustus Stelle,	April, 1864.
Peter A. Runyon,	September, 1875.

THE STELLE GENEALOGY IN PART.

Rev. Benjamin, son of Pontius Stelle, born 1683, married Mercy Drake. Their children were as follows: Mercy, Susanna, Betsy, Benjamin, John, Isaac. Benjamin became a deacon of the Church. John, a Chaplain in the Revolutionary Army; Isaac, a minister of the Gospel, and third pastor of this Church.

Benjamin, son of Rev. Benjamin, born 1783, married first, Hannah Dunn; married second, Ruth Sharp.

Children of first wife. Mary married Andrew Manning.
" " Mercy married Ephraim Piatt
" " Elizabeth married Joseph Stelle.
" " Asher married Mary Drake.
" " Isaac married Margaret Manning.
" " Benjamin.
" " Rachel married Ephraim Fitz Randolph.
Child of second wife. Samuel married Elizabeth Bishop.

Rev. Isaac, son of Rev. Benjamin Stelle, born 1718, married Christiana Clarkson. Their children were:
Benjamin, married Huldah Crawford.
Ambrose.
Abel married Sarah Dunham.
Joseph married Elizabeth Stelle.
Mary.
Mercy.
Oliver, married Mary Runyon.
Samuel married Hannah Taylor.

Descendants of Rev. Benjamin Stelle who have either died or been dismissed by letter within the last fifty years:

Drake Stelle,	Rev. Lewis Stelle,
Daniel Stelle,	Rachel D. Stelle,
Rev. Bergen Stelle,	Prudence Stelle,
Julia A. Stelle,	Sarah Stelle,
Jeremiah D. Stelle,	Rachel Stelle,

The descendants of Rev. Benjamin Stelle, now members of the Church, are :

William H. Stelle,	Bergen D. Stelle,
Sarah J. Letson,	Elsie M. Stelle,
S. Raymond Stelle.	D. E. Stelle.
Wm. T. Stelle,	Mary E. Stelle.
Isabella Stelle,	Anna C. Davis.

Descendants of Rev. Isaac Stelle who have either died or been dismissed within the past fifty years :

Isaac Stelle,	Adaline G. Stelle,
Mary Ann Stelle,	Phœbe D. Stelle,
Elizabeth M. Stelle,	Margaret J. Stelle,
Rachel Stelle,	Rebecca A. Stelle,
Adaline Stelle,	Susanna A. Stelle,
Mahlon Stelle,	Gifford Stelle.
Jas. Patterson Stelle,	Isaac R. Stelle,
Lewis F. Stelle,	Anna E. Stelle,
Augustus T. Stelle,	John N. Stelle,
Samuel R. Stelle.	Susan R. Stelle,
Alexander B. Stelle.	Annie E. Stelle,
James D. Stelle,	Samuel R. Stelle,
Isaac Stelle,	Mahlon C. Stelle,
Prudence Stelle,	Fanny D. Stelle,
George W Stelle,	Mamie A. Stelle,

Lucy Stelle.

Descendants of Rev. Isaac Stelle, now members of the Church :

Sarah Stelle,	Samuel E. Stelle,
Mary A. Stelle,	Almira Stelle,
Isabella D. Stelle,	Isaac D. Stelle.
Alice H. Stelle,	Augustus Stelle,
Louisa R. Stelle,	Angeline Stelle,
Sarah Stelle,	Julia Stelle.

Members of the New Brunswick First Church, descendants of Rev. Isaac Stelle :

Sarah E. Stelle.	Anna Stelle,
Rachel M. Stelle,	Mary Stelle.

Helen Stelle.

ANCESTRY OF REV. REUNE RUNYON.

1. Vincent Runyon or Rongnion married Ann Boutcher, daughter of John Boutcher of Hartford, England, June 28, 1668, in the 20th year of the reign of Charles II. They had five children, but no record of their birth or death appears to exist.

2. Vincent Runyon, son of the foregoing, married Mary Huff____.[1] Had eight children, viz. : Vincent, Reune, Reuben, Reziah, Sarah, Martha, Rizpah and Ann.

[1]. Last name unknown.

3. Reune born 1707, died 1776, married Rachel Drake, born 1711, died 1784. Their children were : Mary, Ephraim, Rachel, Reune, John[1] and Rizpah.

REV. REUNE RUNYON AND HIS DESCENDANTS.

Rev. Reune Runyon, born in Piscataway, November 29, 1741, the son of Reune Runyon and Rachel Drake, married 1765 Anna Bray. Their children were twelve : five dying in childhood, viz. : Rachel, Reuben, Charlotte, Rhoda and Mary.

The seven following lived to be married and had families :

BORN.

1766.—Nancy Runyon married Rev. Geo. Drake ; their children were : Reune, George, Ann, Mary.

1771.—Vincent Runyon married Providence Runyon ; their children were three daughters : Mary, Esther, Elizabeth.

1773.—Rachel Runyon married Jonathan Dayton ; their children were : Jesse, Simeon, Ann, Betsey and Samuel.

1775.—Daniel Runyon married Phebe Runyon and Sarah Holton, their children were : Reune, Peter, Ann, Rhoda, Cornelia, Joseph, Elizabeth.

1777.—Reune B. Runyon married Hudlah Drake, their children were : Oliver, Reune D., Samuel, Juliet. Anna, Mercy, Mary, Rhoda.

1784.—Matilda Runyon married James Tanner.

1786.—Isabel Runyon married John Holton.

The family of Reune B. all married, viz :

Oliver married Rachel Runyon, lived in Plainfield.
Reune D. married Rebecca Brokaw, lived in Newmarket.
Samuel married Sarah Crissey, lived in Piscataway.
Juliet married Louis Runyon, lived in Plainfield.
Anna married Nathan Blackford, lived in Middlesex.
Mercy Married Abel S. Runyon, lived near New Brunswick.
Mary married Henry Crissey.
Rhoda married David Manning, lived in Piscataway.
The family of Daniel married in part, and lived in Plainfield, all of them.

---

1. John, the brother of Rev. Reune Runyon, had a son Ephraim, who was the father of Abraham Runyon, now of Dunellen, who has reached the venerable age of eighty-eight years, and whose children are the distinguished ex-Chancellor Theodore Runyon, of Newark, and Mrs. William C. Stanbury of Scotch Plains. They are therefore the seventh generation in descent from the first Vincent Runyon or Rongnion, who married Ann Boutcher, of Hartford, England.

Exercises

— ON —

Bi-Centennial Day.

THE day appointed for the Bi-Centennial celebration, (June 20, 1889), proved very propitious. The skies were clear, the air pure and bracing, and everything seemed to conspire to elevate the feelings and bring them into joyful harmony with the occasion.

The congregation began to assemble a short time before the hour announced for beginning the service. Each arriving train brought additional visitors, while many from the surrounding country came in their own conveyances. Before the opening exercises were concluded, the church was filled to overflowing and continued so throughout the day and evening. The pulpit and platform were profusely and tastefully decorated with flowers and evergreens. On one side of the alcove there appeared, enclosed in a beautiful wreath, the significant figures "1689," composed of richly tinted flowers, and on the opposite side one similarly arranged containing the figures "1889." The ladies had provided for their guests a bountiful supply of inviting edibles for both dinner and supper, which were served at the large, unoccupied house and grounds opposite the parsonage.

The audience manifested the deepest interest in the entire proceedings at the church, and visitors from far and near expressed their heartiest appreciation of the entertainment afforded them. All connected with the church found the occasion a most delightful and inspiring one—a day never to be forgotten in the history of their beloved Zion.

THE BI-CENTENNIAL SERVICES.

— ‑ ‑ ‑

GREETING BY THE PASTOR,   -   J. W. SARLES, D. D.

In behalf of this church, let me say to the dear friends who are our guests to-day that your presence is grateful. Indeed the antici-pation of your coming, representatives of the great Baptist family of New Jersey and other parts, has entered so fully into our notion of a commemorative service that it would hardly be a Bi-Centennial with-out you.

There are substantial reasons why that should be so. If to us the lines have fallen in pleasant places, so they have to you. If we have a goodly heritage, you have the same. There has been here a long line of noble ancestry. But they were your progenitors as well as ours. The Piscataway Baptist Church is one of the three notable mothers of all New Jersey Baptists, and many more. Our joy to-day therefore is one in common with yours. It was meet that we should invite you here, and that you have come.

Besides that, we gratefully accept it that the children are not un-worthy of the fathers. As in the past so now, men and women of great renown in God's sight are living actors. It was in a moment of great depression that the heroic Elijah once thought that he, already as good as dead, was the very last of the faithful on earth. At that instant there were seven thousand who were true to Israel's God. The Great Head of the Church is never wanting for such ; and we are, making constant acknowledgements of it a year too late. Our annual letters to the Associations are all crowded with loving words appre-ciative of those who have been taken from us. To many of those, poor in spirit, that just recognition would have been a grateful sur-prise,—" When saw we Thee an hungered and fed Thee,"—awaken-ing new gratitude, inspiring new confidence, and nerving for the last conflict, while only faintly foreshadowing what the Master himself will say. Many dear Christians have slipped away while I have been getting to the point of telling them what blessings God has made them to me. Tens of thousands of the "called and chosen faithful" are now on the earth, and among them hosts of Baptists, "partners and fellow-helpers" of the Apostles, "messengers of the churches and the glory of Christ." Many of these are sure to be found in such a gathering as this. To look upon them is a privilege; to wait upon them a joy ; to honor them a delight. All this is ours to-day.

Of the noble men and women who founded this Church, and stood by it unfalteringly through manifold trials, and who passed it, a sacred trust, along down from sire to son, from mother to daughter, of these you will hear in the history prepared for this occasion. All honor to them, as appointed by God: "Them that honor me I will honor." Because of His mighty grace in them, and His over-shadowing presence with them, all this ground on which we are gathered is holy ground. From the time they first owned a habitation, they stood and served on the identical spot where we are now assembled. This hill is and ought to be held sacred. The names of these heroes of faith are " as ointment poured forth ;" their "memory blessed." What an indulgence it would be to say in their presence what is in our hearts. We shall, by and by. In the meantime, we will not lose the opportunity of having a word with their descendants, and telling them to their face what we think of them. Equal honors to the noble men and women and children who to-day stand as honestly, as wholeheartedly, as self-denyingly as unfalteringly, and as cheerfully for the same great principles, annointed by one and the self same mighty Spirit. To say that we welcome you is not the expression that our hearts seek. We invited you. You have made us glad by your coming, and we feel honored with your company. If it were given to us to make some substantial return, our cup would run over. If our hearts were so inflamed with Christ's love, that we could not look you in the face, take your hand or speak without ministering grace to you, that return would fittingly follow such a two hundred years of grace. Our prayer has been and is that your coming may be the occasion when the Holy Spirit shall suddenly come upon you and upon us, and so, bring times of refreshing to all the churches here represented.

The best we have, sanctuary, sacred precincts, homes and all, we put into your hands.

ADDRESS BY   -   -   REV. E. EVERETT JONES.

Pastor of the Middletown Baptist Church.

The old Middletown Baptist Church sends cordial greetings to the Piscataway Church on this, her festive day and two hundredth birthday. At the centennial commencement of North Carolina University, held this week, among other interesting exercises, the papers tell us, there were a number of class re-unions, and among them the "Class of '24 " was the first to answer to the roll-call ; that, touching beyond expression was it to see men with silvery locks and infirm steps—"boys of seventy-five and eighty-five summers"—living their school days over again and telling of playing pranks on professors and freshmen, and growing enthusiastic over their college belles of more than sixty years ago. So, to-day, some of us, as the representatives of the oldest Baptist Church in New Jersey, come to congratulate, and call up the past historic lore in mutual stimulus and delight. Sometimes at happy family reunions, some of the brothers or sisters may be unavoidably deprived of the pleasures of the occasion and can only send by dear ones their messages of love. To-day, the elder sister from Middletown cannot be present, and hence sends up her latest addition in pastoral ranks to bear her tributes of heartfelt affection to her younger sister.

The extraordinary occasion—the two hundredth anniversary of the organization of a Baptist Church—which calls us together, awakens interesting thoughts of various kinds.

In the first place, age itself naturally awakens our respect and throws the character of dignity over men and things. A Greek historian tells us how, in the pure and early and most virtuous days of the republic of Greece, if an old man entered the crowded assembly, all ranks rose to give room and place to him. Age also throws a character of dignity over all—even over inanimate objects—so that spectators regard them with a sort of awe and reverence. You will stand before the hoary and ivy-mantled ruins of some castle of a bye-gone age, with deeper feelings of respect than ever touched you in the marbled halls or amid the gilded grandeur of modern palaces. Nor does the proudest tree that ever lifts its head and towering form to the skies, affect you with such strange emotions as some old, withered, wasted trunk of a tree, hollowed by time into a gnarled shell, still showing some green and signs of life.

2. Pride of ancestry is another line of thought which stirs our hearts to-day. As the Grecian maiden, when asked "What fortune she would bring her husband?" replied: "A heart unspotted and virtue without a stain." The inheritance from parents who both had these, and nothing else to leave—the inheritance of noble ancestry, tried and true, pure and sure, is a priceless boon. Many a parent has only been able to leave his children his good name, and that was very much to them. Likewise, this old Church may well point with finger of natural and laudable pride to-day to a noble ancestry, and a grand religious ancestry, more particularly.

Said that eminent Scotch divine, Dr. Thomas Guthrie: "As far as I can trace my ancestors, I claim to be of the seed of the righteous." A higher honor, surely, than all the boasted noble blood of the world. A great thing it is to be descended from those who "earnestly contended for the faith once delivered to the saints," and even when persecuted for righteousness sake.

Heredity is a subject greatly discussed in recent years, but some great facts in the matter certainly stand out in bold relief, like the peaks in the mountains.

If the Imperial House of Hapsburgh, since the marriage some few centuries ago with the Polish family of Gagellon, has had decidedly peculiar features ; if the royal family of England has had peculiar lateral parts of the face from George I. to Victoria ; if the Bruces of Scotland have all the strongly marked features of face, which appear on the coins of that heroic monarch ; if the prevalent tallness of the people of Potsdam, descended from the tall guards of Frederick I ; if the Spanish features of the people of the county of Galway, where Spanish settlements were made centuries ago ; and, if the hereditary beauty of the women of Prague are all well-known facts, and have frequently attracted the attention of chronologists ; yea ! if the Jewish physiognomies on the sepulchral monuments of Egypt are identical with those observed among modern Jews on the streets of any great city, then there must be more in heredity than we have ever yet explored. Why, then, is it not equally plain that the religious tenets of ancestry will generally prevail with their descendants ? And if they be found in strict accord with Scripture, how great an honor to them also. Great influence have parents, and through them their parents and ancestors before them. Their opinions, their spirit, their converse, their manners, their example and their religious views, particularly, all mightily influence. Is it not an honor to be descended from the persecuted Biblemen of former ages—from the Albigenses and Waldenses, or from Baptists generally, " earnestly contending for the faith " ? or from the faithful Baptists of Piscataqua— the Dunns, Drakes, Smalleys, Dunhams, Randolphs or Fitz-Randolphs, Stelles, Mannings, Runyons, Blackfords, Walkers, Daytons, and many other old-time Baptist names ?

3.   Good name of one's own coining, however, is even far more honorable than any pride of descent from noble ancestry.   Hermodius, the descendant of a great ancient family, once spoke disparagingly of Iphrecrates, a famous general of old, because of his humble birth, he having been the son of a shoemaker.   But his reply was : " My nobility begins in me, but yours ends in you."   Far grander thing is it indeed to have nobility and great good name, in Church or one's own self, along the record made, than merely to don the laurels of noble progenitors.   Ah ! that invisible thing called " good name," made up of the breath of great numbers who' speak well of us, is really choicest possession. Whilst eager pursuit of empty applause is vain, and nothing more so ; yet, good name to any one or any cause is the sweet perfume borne along with it and its success and scattered wherever it works, is the very crowning glory of it.   It thus becomes a tower of strength, a mighty name, shedding light on darkness, breathing life into cold forms, and like Pharoah's signet ring on Joseph's hand of old, is endued with sovereign influence and power.   As for the historic record of this old church for two hundred years, it is good, entirely good and nothing but good.

> " Good name is dear to all :
> Is the immediate jewel of the soul :
> Whole kingdoms, life, were given for it, and he
> Who got it, was the winner still."

4.   Usefulness, however, is the criterion of glory, according to the New Testament teachings.   If any would be chief, let him minister unto all.

In the school of Pythagorus, it was a point of discipline that if any among the probationists grew weary of studying to be useful, they were to be regarded as dead, and funeral obsequies were to be performed for them, and tombs were to be raised for them with inscriptions to warn others of the like mortality. Thus would they quicken them to refine their souls above such a wretched state. But never has the old Piscataway Church seemed to grow weary of studying to be useful. The benevolent and missionary contributions of over $1,500 last year, in the State Convention Minutes, alone considered, is an abundant attestation. It evidently is a busy Gospel hive. When Dr. Lyman Beecher was laboring most successfully in Boston, he was asked how it was he was able to accomplish so much. Said he : " It is not I, but my Church. I preach as hard as I can on Sabbath, and then I have four hundred members who go out and preach every day of the week." Thus success perched upon their banners, and thus they went forth as an army with banners.

5. But beyond all else, constancy seems to have been the great balance-wheel and cardinal virtue through the two centuries of the history of this Church. It has continued two hundred years, active, steadfast, persevering, and stronger than ever. Men of business oft place up in prominent places the date when their business was established, to show how long it has continued and to prove how reliable and successful it has been, and thus claim to be worthy of all confidence.

At Wittenberg, under a gothic canopy upon a pedestal of polished granite, stands a bronze figure of Martin Luther, with his gown and bands, and the Bible in his arms. Upon the base of the monument is the inscription : " If it is God's work, it will stand ; but if it is man's work, it will perish." Since that day, ever-spreading Protestantism is his noblest monument. Likewise of this old church. It has stood two hundred years as a monument to the work of its worthies gone before, and as evidencing its founding and work has been of God. Thus remarkable record has been made, and record, too, of greatest influence. But nothing takes place without leaving traces behind it, and in many cases so distinct as to leave no doubt of their cause. In the material world events testify of themselves to future ages. If we were to visit some unknown region and behold masses of lava covered with soil, with different degrees of thickness, we should certainly have a persuasion of remote and successive volcanic eruptions, as if we had lived in the ages when they took place. Similarly do the great civil and religious movements and conquests leave equally their impressions on society—leave institutions, manners, and a variety of monuments. So this old Church has been instrumental, under God, of filling up all the surrounding country with Baptists and Baptist churches, and even out in all directions, far and near, as a mother and grandmother of many churches. And now at last, these three old sister churches of New Jersey—Middletown, of 1688 ; Piscataway of 1689, and Cohansey of 1690—stand out before us in beauteous attitude, like "three sister islands" in the great river of Time, bathed in the mists of His love, radiant with the beams of His smile, and reflecting a heavenly splendor over all the surrounding Christian world.

ADDRESS BY   -   -   -   J. H. PARKS. D.D.

Pastor of the Scotch Plains Baptist Church.

Rev. Dr. J. H. Parks spoke substantially as follows: I am glad to be present on this interesting occasion and to represent the Scotch Plains Baptist Church in extending greetings and congratulations to "Mother Piscataway"—we are proud of our parentage, and grateful to God for the history of the Mother Church. Christian churches are in some respects like lighthouses—they are placed where they are most needed—they are founded upon the rock, and they are built and sustained in order that they may let the light shine. How well the old Piscataway Church has fulfilled its mission in this regard, let facts and remembrances to-day determine.

Christian churches are like recruiting offices in the kings army. They are established for the enlisting of soldiers who shall do efficient service, even in the time of hand to hand encounter—and we gladly and gratefully recall in the two centuries past many a veteran of the cross, who has bravely stood up for Jesus, and defended the truth, who was enlisted at the Piscataway recruiting station.

Christian churches are like training schools where men are qualified for efficiency, drilled and disciplined for positions to which they are best adapted. And all the churches in this whole vicinity have received members from this training school of our Lord Jesus.

Christian churches are like families who live not only for themselves, but who rear and send out children, who organize other families and thus multiply the household of faith.

The Scotch Plains Baptist Church is the eldest daughter of the Piscataway Church, organized in 1747, and has been an independent family ever since. The daughter has behaved pretty well during the whole one hundred and forty-two years of her life. Only fifteen years after her organization she reported a membership of 140, and there has not been a year since, when her number has been less than that. She has given birth to four children who, of course, became grandchildren of the Piscataway Church. The First Baptist Church of New York city which is noted for its solid substantial record, and its broad influence—the Lyons Farm Church—the Mount Bethel Church, and the new Brooklyn Church; all of whom are reliable both in doctrine and in practice.

The Scotch Plains Church is in condition just now to thank God and take courage; and they hope the time may come, in the near future, when they will be enabled to do broader evangelical work than ever they have done before.

We have reason as Baptists to-day to praise the Great Head in Zion for the influence of the Piscataway Church upon our denominational history in this commonwealth. May the future be even more successful than the past has been, and conduce in still greater degree to the glory of our Sovereign Master.

Bi-centennial Hymn by - ABRAHAM COLES, L.L.D.

Prepared by request especially for this occasion.

Praise to Christ, the Everliving,
    Who, Two Hundred years ago,
Planted here a vine, and made it
    In a virgin soil to grow ;
With His own hands pruned and dressed it,
    Made it blossom and bear fruit,
Frosts of Winter did not harm it
    For His life was at the root.

Dear to God, the climbing wonder,
    Herb of grace and plant of fame !—
Ever bearing purple clusters
    To the honor of His name ;
Glory of the Master's garden,—
    Its chief ornament and pride !
When much fruit bends down the branches
    How the Lord is glorified !

Brief on earth is man's existence,
    Naught continues in one stay—
Change on change, the fatal morrow
    Wrecks the promise of to-day.
'Mid the throes of revolution,
    Rise of kingdoms and their fall,
This survives, and long shall flourish
    By thy favor, Lord of All !

Address by   -   -   REV. ADDISON PARKER,
Pastor of the Morristown Baptist Church.

It was a hundred and thirty-seven years ago that your second daughter set up housekeeping for herself. I take it as an indication of the breadth of its early influence that the Piscataway Church in 1752 should have had eleven members, seven men and four women living nearly twenty-five miles away, across three ranges of hills, and beyond the great swamp, whom it could dismiss, to unite with six others to form the church at Morristown.

The representatives of this church greet you to-day. We rejoice to be permitted to pay our tribute of respect to a body so venerable

in years, so honorable in record, so sterling in virtues, and so benefi-
cent in influence.

The Church at Morristown was planted in a region then sparsely
settled, but already strongly pre-occupied by another denomination,
which for a hundred years following held dominant religious influence.

It is a region where Baptists always have had to labor at a disad-
vantage. To whatever else the Baptists of our State have held they
do not seem to have been given to ultra montanism. Very few of
them comparatively have ever gone beyond the mountains into the
heart of Northern New Jersey.

Necessarily the beginning of the Church was small, until recent
years its growth was slow. Its constituency was widely scattered over
the outlying farms and hamlets of the region. Preaching stations and
branches are mentioned at different times at Rockaway, Paruppany,
Littleton, New Vernon and Schooley's Mountain ; places distant from
Morristown from four to ten and fifteen miles. The location of the
Church for the first sixteen years was in a small building about two
miles to the south of Morristown. Then it moved into town and
built a meeting-house upon the village green. This house of worship
stood for sixty-six years. It was replaced by another upon the same
site, that has twice since been enlarged and reconstructed, and that
soon will give place, after nearly half a century of use, to a structure
more accordant with the needs of the Church and the demands of the
times.

An idea of its early estate may be gotten from the stipends paid
to some of its preachers. The first pastor had a salary of two hundred
dollars a year. Elder Van Horn, the Pastor at Scotch Plains, preached
once a month at Morristown for fifteen years. He was paid a hundred
and fifty dollars.

Money went further in those days. In 1786 Esq. John Brookfield
boarded the preacher. Evidently he was a man of standing. Note
the " Esquire." The Church paid him a dollar a week for the service;
who could not live on a hundred and fifty dollars a year, with board
at a dollar a week ?

It is evident that a measure of prosperity attended the early
history of the Church. A hundred years ago, when it was thirty-six
years old, it had eighty-nine members, and ranked numerically the
eighth in the list of the twenty-four churches we then had in the State.

Had that rate of advance continued it would long ago have
become a strong congregation. Such was not the case. For long
periods its condition was stationary, or else on the decline.

The war of the Revolution and the years of confusion and religious declension by which it was followed, bore with peculiar severity
upon its fortunes. Its meeting-house was turned into a store-house
and hospital for the Continental Army in its winter quarters at Morristown ; its people were scattered and its services broken up.

At a later time, in the early part of this century, the Church suffered great depletion from the extreme Calvinism that then left its frost
blight upon so many of our churches in that northern part of the State.

Though it remained true, its Pastor, a man greatly loved, withdrew from its fellowship on account of their views, after having led many to his way of thinking. These parties withdrew from their Church obligations through a firm belief that the Church had departed from its true faith in entering on missionary and similar enterprises. They called it "going after the beast."

The members were reduced to thirty-five, only two of them residing in town and only six of them men.

After these days of sore trial there came a gradual but marked improvement, which has gone on now for more than half a century, and especially within the last eight years, in which more than a hundred converts have been baptized and the effective strength of the Church has been more than doubled. So far as contributions are a test of strength, your second child now stands among the first twelve of our churches in the State.

The Morristown Church has been fortunate in its pastors. It counts as one of its choicest honors the fact that it was permitted to ordain as its first pastor one who became the most eloquent and influential Baptist clergyman of his day, John Gano—"shone like a star of the first magnitude." The child is the father of the man; the young preacher of the matured one. A single incident lingers in tradition about his work in Morristown. A poor colored woman had professed conversion and asked to be baptized, but for some reason was repeatedly put off by the pastor, until she began to dispair. One day in going out of Church she began to mutter about her hopeless estate, "What was the matter," asked the friends? She said she had had a dream. She thought she had died and gone up to the gate of Heaven. The angel asked where she came from? "From Morristown." "What Church do you belong to? "I don't belong to any Church, for that little Johnny Gano won't baptize me." Just then Mr. Gano came laong, "Here," said he, "you shall not have it to say I kept you out of Heaven. If you want so much to be baptized I will baptize you."

He was the man who when a chaplain in the army, going one morning to pray with his regiment passed a group of officers, one of whom was swearing most profanely. "Good morning, Doctor," said the swearing Lieutenant. "Good morning, sir," replied the Chaplain. "You pray early this morning?" "I beg your pardon, sir." "Oh, I cannot pardon you; bring your case to God."

Rev. Reune Runyon, another of its early pastors whom it ordained to his work, was a licentiate of the mother Church of Piscataway, and went from Morristown after six years of faithful service to assume the pastorate of the Church of his nativity. We remember to day that we have given something to you as well as we have received from you. I said the Church has been fortunate in its ministry. Many humble but devoted souls have laid themselves upon the alter of its service, whose work God knows better than man. Others have gone out to broader fields. A Church that has given pastors to the First Church, New York, like John Gano; to Piscataway, like Reune Runyon, to to first Newark, like Sym; to Elizabeth, like Turton; to Rahway, like

Tolan ; to Madison Avenue, New York, like Bridgeman ; to Bunker
Hill, Boston, like Morse; to Norwalk, like Bentley ; to Harvard street,
Boston, like Gunning ; to Waltham, like Stratton, may well delight to
hold their success with those of many others less conspicuous, but not
less worthy, in grateful memory.

The times change—

> " The old order faileth, changing to the new,"
> " And God fulfils himself in many ways."

In change let there be progress. From the backward glance let
us turn our faces to the brighter sunshine of coming days.

ADDRESS BY   -   -   **J. W. WILLMARTH, D.D.,**

Moderator of the Philadelphia Baptist Association.

MY DEAR BROTHER SARLES AND MY CHRISTIAN FRIENDS :

I consider it a high honor to represent the Philadelphia Association at the bi-centennial of this ancient Church. Since you left us we
have gone on increasing ; new Associations have been formed, and yet
to-day we number ninety-one churches and had, last October, 27,083
members. Our Association is indeed too large. I bring you the warm
and hearty greetings of the Philadelphia Baptist Association—"the
mother of us all"—with our best wishes for your future growth and
prosperity. In these fraternal greetings and wishes I believe that every
minister and every member of our body would join with one accord.

What a change since, two hundred years ago, this Church was
organized ; or since, one hundred and eighty-one years ago, the Philadelphia Association was formed by five little churches—three in New
Jersey, one in Pennsylvania and one in Delaware—Middletown, Piscataway, Cohansey, Pennepek and Welch Tract! Then these colonies con-
sisted only of a few settlements on the fringe of a vast wilderness. The
great and opulent cities of to-day were little towns or had no existence,
and the colonists were under the sway—often tyrannical—of the mother
country. The genial soil and government of New Jersey attracted those
from all quarters who desired to make for themselves happy homes,
free from oppression and persecution ; yet it was emphatically a new
country, and the barbarous Indian lingered among the settlers looking
with stupid wonder on a rising civilization which, he had not the mind
to comprehend or the will to imitate.

The Baptists of those days were a " feeble folk." A few little
churches here and there, liable to bitter persecution, except in Rhode
Island, New Jersey, Pennsylvania and Maryland ; and whether persecuted or not, they were of so little account in the eyes of the great
world as to be hardly deemed worthy of notice. Yet, clearly under-

standing those scriptural principles which it was not given to the great ones of church and state to receive or to respect, our denominational ancestors held these principles tenaciously and consistently. They were true to the truth at any cost. They would have sealed their testimony with their blood.

To-day, behold this great republic, one of the mightiest powers of earth, stretching from the Atlantic to the Pacific, and from the Polar snows to the tropic seas ! The home of sixty millions of people ; it is filled with energy, enterprise and progress. I believe that our country has been preserved through many dangers and conflicts, that it may be the place where great problems of human welfare and of redemption may find room and scope for being worked out fittingly and on a vast scale. By no accident have these United States become such a favored nation, with such singular advantages of position, soil, freedom, and every element of greatness.

The Baptists have had a growth here that is simply marvelous. Their numbers run into the millions, and their wealth, power, learning and influence are such as our fathers never dreamed of. Our principles, once bitterly scorned, have been adopted in part by almost all Protestant Christians in Europe and America. The battle is not over ; but religious liberty has completely triumphed here, and is advancing to a complete triumph in Europe. Several pedobaptist denominations, by a happy inconsistency, require evidence of conversion in order to full membership, and if we hold fast to the faith delivered once for all to the saints and testify to the truth in word and· deed, it would seem that the time must be at hand when God's scattered and divided children shall become one flock.

What is there before us? Oh! an impenetrable veil hides the future from our vision, and we have no gift of prophecy that might enable us to draw it back and foretell what is to be in the days to come. But we know that principles will work themselves out in their appropriate lines ; that like causes will produce like effects ; that all things follow their tendencies.

Will our Baptist churches be able to stem the tide of worldliness ? They have grown great under the sharp discipline of persecution, reproach and poverty. Will they withstand the severer trials and temptations born of wealth, affluence and peace? Will they hold fast to all the truth as firmly as they maintain immersion? Will they resist all tendencies of the " New Theology" and the " Down Grade"? Will they cling with undiminished faith to the absolute inspiration of the Scriptures, to the divinity and atonement of Jesus, and to the doctrines of Sovereign Grace—those great truths, often called Calvinistic, which are the very heart and strength of Christianity ? Will they resist the subtle temptation to practically abandon their distinctive tenet of the absolute separation of Church and State—of the spiritual and secular spheres ? Will they remember that the Church is a spiritual body, commanded to seek purely spiritual ends by exclusively spiritual means ? Will they refuse the tempter's insidious and plausible suggestion that we may now rule, reform and regenerate the world, if the Church will only call for the help of magistrates and legislators, and will earnestly engage in political strife?

On the answer which we shall give to such questions depends the future of our beloved denomination. Here the ways part—the way to grander growth, greater purity and mightier power, and the way to decadence, feebleness and apostasy.

I am no prophet—I cannot foresee what of good or evil the next hundred or two hundred years will bring to us, if indeed the Lord does not come. But I know that so long as the present age shall last, He will always have a seed to serve Him, a people chosen from the beginning to salvation through sanctification of the Spirit and belief of the truth. I know that He will always have His faithful witnesses who will proclaim His truth and if need be, suffer for it. I know that sooner or later He will come in glory, to establish his kingdom—to renew the heavens and the earth and to put his people in possession of their inheritance. I know that if we follow Him faithfully and die before He comes, we shall enter at once upon the higher life and with Him joyfully wait for the grand consummation. Let us, then, be of good courage and serve our Lord with a true heart and with supreme devotion.

> Beyond the veil of blinded sense
> The Risen One builds our residence ;
> There may we meet some golden day
> And live and love in bliss for aye.

ADDRESS BY - - ḦOṆ. ḦORẠTIO GẠTES JOṆES,

President of Trustees of the Philadelphia Association.

I, too, with my respected associate, Rev. Dr. Willmarth, feel most highly honored in having been invited by your venerable Church to participate in your bi-centennial services. Dr. Willmarth, the moderator of our Association, has well stated the exact position we now occupy, and it scarcely seems necessary that I should say anything more. But having been connected with that ancient body, through my father and my grandfather and my cousins Abel and Enoch Morgan, Benjamin Griffith and Obadiah Holmes, for one hundred and seventy-nine years, it gives me most peculiar pleasure to be with you to-day.

For twenty-two years I have been President of our corporation, and, as you may suppose, feel a deep interest in all that pertains to our Baptist Zion. For New Jersey I have a special regard, as my grandfather, Rev. David Jones, the chaplain of General Wayne during the Revolution and the Indian wars of 1794–6, was a student at Isaac Eaton's Academy at Hopewell, the first Baptist Academy in America, and gave to Rhode Island College its first president, the Rev. Dr. James Manning.

I also look upon New Jersey, and especially upon the Middletown Church, with a kind of sentimental affection, for while studying Divinity under his cousin, Abel Morgan, my grandfather fell in love—a habit I believe still quite common among theological students of the present day— with a handsome young lady named Anne Stillwell, who was a descendant of the martyr Obadiah Holmes, who in 1651 was cruelly whipped on Boston Common for having preached the Gospel at Lynn, without any authority from the "Standing Order" of Massachusetts Bay. Is it any wonder, Mr. Chairman, that to-day I feel proud of New Jersey?

And now, as I heard you intimate when introducing me, you wish me to tell you what we of the Philadelphia Association have been doing since the Piscataway Church in 1792 joined the New York Association. Well, sir, we have endeavored to keep the faith as it was once delivered to the saints. We have tried to hold fast the truths of the Gospel as contained in the Confession of Faith adopted by us in 1742. We have not followed cunningly devised fables, and if any of our ministers chance to do so, we let them go, and they are seldom heard of afterwards.

When you left us we had in our Association fifty-three churches, and now we have ninety-one. Then we had 3,253 members, now we have 27,083. Since then we organized in Philadelphia the Baptist Triennial Convention, now the Missionary Union, but Jersey took an active part in that convention. We have also formed there the American Baptist Publication Society, whose colporteurs and books are to be found in nearly every State of the Union ; we have also founded the Lewisburg (now Bucknell) University, and at Upland, near Philadelphia, we have The Crozer Theological Seminary, with an endowment fund of $351,000. What have we done ? Why, my dear brother, we have formed academies and schools throughout the State, and in our Association we have a "Building Fund" to lend money to feeble churches without interest, repaying ten per cent. of the principal each year, and also a "Ministers' and Widows' Fund," for the care and support of needy Ministers and their Widows, and we have also the Baptist Home, of Philadelphia, where we now have over seventy needy Baptist women ; and we also have a Baptist Orphanage. Besides these, we have at Germantown an institution called "The George Nugent Home for Baptists," founded by that noble man of God, George Nugent, the senior deacon of the Second Baptist Church of Germantown, where Baptist ministers and their wives over the age of sixty years, *from any State of the Union*, can find a home. It is my pleasure to refer to this, because I am Trustee under the will of Mr. Nugent, and President of the Board of Trustees of the Home. These are only a few of the good things we have been doing since you left us in 1792.

And now, Mr. Chairman, I think my time is up, and yet I would like to know what the Piscataway Church has been doing since 1792. I have listened very attentively to what my old friend and college classmate, James Fuller Brown, D. D., has been telling about your Church. You have done great good and have had considerable trouble about trifling matters—a very natural state of affairs in this state of probation

One chief trouble was on the question of marrying a deceased wife's sister. Is there anything in the New Testament on the subject? If not, then why say that we are bound by the Jewish laws? In our Association we do not now trouble ourselves about such matters. If members of our churches choose to marry ladies old enough to be their grandmothers, we don't censure them for so doing, believing they will sooner or later find they have made a grand mistake.

But, Mr. Chairman, my time is more than up, and I must close. I tender to you and your Church my best wishes for your prosperity in all future time. To me this day has been one of joy, because I have seen so many dear friends ; and yet of sadness, for I know that most of us will never meet again.

My brethren and sisters, as I have listened to the organ's notes filling this house and dying away in the far off distance—as I have heard the voices of the choir blending their sweet songs in unison, I have fancied that there were echoes from the music of other lands unseen. I have almost felt there were angelic bands around us to-day—bands of the sainted dead who once met in this hallowed spot, striking their celestial harps and sending forth sweet and heavenly strains,

> " Like the sound of a host on their homeward march,
> The songs of their Fatherland singing."

ADDRESS BY   -   -   - REV. A. ARMSTRONG.

Pastor of the New Brooklyn Baptist Church.

The Samptown Baptist Church was constituted 1792 by twenty-one members drawing letters from the Scotch Plains Church for that purpose. It had at that time, and for many years a large territory as its field, and was much prospered. Subsequently by the growth of Plainfield, New Market and Dunelen, its field became circumscribed, and no growth of population in its locality—congregations depleted. A colony went out for the constitution of Plainfield Baptist Church, and in 1852 another colony went out to form the New Market Church. And from this date for some twenty years there was gradual decline and the brethren became much discouraged. In August, 1878, Rev. A. Armstrong was called to the pastorate. And as the Lord would have it the old edifice took fire from a passing locomotive on Wednesday, April 25th, 1879, and in two hours it was reduced to ashes. The Church and pastor gathered up courage, and having an insurance upon the old house of $2,000, started a subscription and very soon found it safe to secure a lot in New Brooklyn, upon which a new edifice was erected and paid for. And the congregation entered its new home on January 1st, 1880. The Church, with new house in a new location, dropped the name Samptown, which seemed without any significance, and took the corporate name of New Brooklyn. The Church has taken on new life and activity, and experienced a good degree of prosperity—is up with the times in its work of benevolence—and promptly meets all financial responsibilities with satisfaction and pleasure.

It has pleased the Lord to grant a very precious and powerful work of grace this year (1889), there have been added to the Church fellowship forty-four persons, twenty-eight of whom were received by baptism.

The Church by her delegates to this your Bi-centennial, sends greeting and congratulation upon your green old age of vitality and great prosperity, hoping that the loving fraternity that has so long existed between daughter and grandmother, may abide and increase as the years go by.

Address by - - REV. H. C. APPLEGARTH, JR.

Pastor of the New Brunswick First Baptist Church.

My Brother Pastor, and Sisters and Brethren of the Piscataway Church :

I count myself happy to be the bearer of the hearty greetings of your third daughter now seventy-three (73) years of age. In common with all your children, she would rise to call you blessed, on this the bi-centennial anniversary of your natal day. Venerable and increased in years you are, but not decrepit. Age has touched you not to enfeeble, but rather to ripen in all noble qualities and graces. We are proud of you, and, though the lines of time have furrowed your once fair face, they make that face none the less, but all the more charming, because they are the beautiful tracery of love—a love which has spent and is spending itself in doing good.

Reviewing your history of two hundred years, and noticing the constancy with which you have maintained the integrity of the truth once delivered to the saints, and also considering the remarkable fact that these twenty decades are girdled with but eleven pastorates—the fact itself being eloquent of praise for your steadfastness—we look upon you to-night as "a tree planted by the rivers of waters, bringing forth fruit in your season ; your leaf also not withering and prospering in whatsoever you do." So, in the grace of our Heavenly Father, may it ever be ! Because, then, of what you are and of what you have done, your third daughter gladly honors you on this glad occasion. And, it may be, you are not altogether ashamed of your daughter. She has endeavored to do virtuously, and, though she has not excelled, she has not totally failed.

We have three children and a baby ; three white and one black, and we glory in the life of our colored child.

Beginning life in a place preoccupied by another denomination, tethered by apparently unyielding circumstances, and obliged, consequently, to work between narrow lines, we have sought to hang the glory of our Christian life upon all surroundings; and, now, it may be interesting to you to know that, as the result of our work in that neighboring city, where our lot is cast, we, to-night, number one in every nineteen of the population.

Your third child herself has grown from a little one to be 575 members strong, and has been enabled during these years to contribute to the doing of the Lord's work in the world about $700,000.

We did not go far from home, nor are we ashamed to be told that we are tied to our mother's apron strings. We staid by you, not because we were afraid to go away, but because we loved you and wanted to be near you, and we can truly say that, "The lines have fallen unto us in pleasant places; yea, we have a goodly heritage." But whatever we have been permitted to do in the great cause of our Lord, we are conscious of our indebtedness to you, and gratefully acknowledge it. We were well born and we glory in our ancestry. The seed, no larger than a grain of mustard, which was sown here two hundred years ago, has grown to be a great tree, and we are only one of the branches. We did not bear the stock, the stock bore us; and to the stock belongs the praise we so gladly bring to you to-night.

But it ill becomes me to occupy more time, knowing how full is the program of exercises for this evening. Let me, in conclusion, wish for you and for ourselves a future more glorious, in every good word and work than we have known in the past, bright and blessed as that past has been.

ADDRESS BY   -   -   -   **D. J. YERKES, D.D.**

Pastor of the Plainfield First Baptist Church.

BRETHREN AND FRIENDS:

It is a real and great pleasure to me to be here to speak in behalf of the First Church of Plainfield, and to bring to you her congratulations on this bi-centennial occasion. With others, children, grandchildren and great grandchildren, we come to sit at the family board. We come to give honor to the already honored mother and to join our thanks with hers to God for His mercy to her and to us. And while we all are happy in being here, you also must be glad that your children have come home and gathered about the old hearthstone to talk about the good old times and to tell you of the ways of the Lord with them.

When children are born to them and the responsibilities of family life are felt by the married pair, they have an anxious solicitude for the little ones that play and prattle about the house. However happy in their children, their loving care for them makes burdens,—burdens it is pleasant to bear. But as the children grow older the burdens become heavier, for then the parents are concerned that the children may be of upright character and well settled in life, and if the parents be Christians that they may serve and honor God. And then when the family circles are widened the old folks who have become grand parents and great grand parents, take the little ones into their hearts and very likely, as they forecast the future of these, it is to them filled with gloomy forebodings.

But no happier lot falls to parents in this world than to see their children and their children's children well to do in life—happily settled and walking in the fear of God. Therefore you ought to be happy to-day when your children and their children come to greet you, for since they went out from the old home to set up housekeeping and to do for themselves, they have followed in your example, have kept the faith as you have kept it, tried to serve the Master as you have served Him, and not one of them has brought reproach upon the honored family name.

We greet you on this the two hundredth anniversary of your existence. Mighty changes have taken place in the world within these two hundred years. Things that were have changed. Some have passed away—governments, opinions, doctrines. New things have come, had their day and are gone, but here is this old Church the same still, with all the strength of fresh and vigorous life. In the moral and religious world age does not signify decay. The old things are not the dying things. They last and grow old because of the power of life within them that resists decay. New things come and go because they have not strength to survive the conflicts that try them. And the new things that last, do so because they have ability to resist decay and change, have capacity to grow *old*. We have old hymns and tunes which generations of our fathers have sung, and they are old just because there is something in them that made them last. The blessed doctrines of grace are old, because the truths of God which they hold have kept them alive in the hearts and faith of His people. Therefore it is that the good old age of this mother Church is not suggestive of approaching dissolution, but of the power of that life from which come the freshness and strength of perpetual youth. .

This people have built new houses of worship, moving from the old into the new. Godly ministers have labored and died among them, and some left them for other fields; generations of men who worshipped on this spot have died, but the Church remains with power unabated, her faith established, her hope undimmed, and still holding forth the word of life. The faith she has kept has kept her. Had she denied the faith, the breath of spiritual life had left her long ago and she would now be dead. But "built on the foundation of the prophets and apostles, Christ Jesus Himself being the chief corner stone," she has continued to live and will live by the power of the living Christ.

The Church for which I speak was organized 1818. There have been upon her roll of membership about 1,800 members. The present membership is over 800. The Church has had during the seventy-one years of her existence only four pastors, Jacob Randolph, Daniel T. Hill, Simeon J. Drake and the present pastor. The Church has followed the mother Church in the matter of long pastorates. And from you the First Church at Plainfield has derived a strain of noble blood. On our Church rolls are the Randolphs, Drakes, Mannings, Runyons, Dunns, Stelles, Boices, Smalleys, Brokaws and others of the old Piscataway stock. And from time to time you have replenished our Church with the blood of a right royal lineage, and we are glad to say that no church was ever blessed with truer, better men and women than some among us who have borne these honored names.

Nor would we forget that we have received a goodly heritage in the sound doctrine which you have transmitted to your posterity. It is ours by direct line through the Samptown and Scotch Plains churches, both of whom have kept it uncontaminated. The Lord is our only Lord and Master and his word our only rule of doctrine and practice, and yet the truth as you have held it through all these years, has proclaimed the right way of the Lord. That is the truth to which we hold. And one fact is worthy of mention—that two men, Jacob Randolph and Simeon J. Drake, who did so much to establish the Church in doctrine were of Piscataway stock. May we all, mother and children stand fast in the faith once delivered to the saints—fight the good fight of faith, run the race set before us, keep the faith—ambitious for no crown save the crown of righteousness which the Lord shall give to all them that love his appearing.

ADDRESS BY   -   -   REV. J. A. CUBBERLEY.

Pastor of the New Market Baptist Church.

Mr. Chairman and kind friends: It is with sincere pleasure that I bear to you on this occasion the hearty congratulations of the Church which I serve. It is surely a momentous epoch in your history. I have read of a wonderful grape vine in the grounds of the palace of Hampton Court, near London, which is over one hundred years old; and for all that time it has not ceased growing and burdening itself yearly with numerous clusters of fruit.

Here is a vine a branch of the living vine, which is two hundred years old, nor has it, taking its history as a whole, ever ceased growing and bearing fruit.

It has outlived successive generations of men, and thus on earth the spiritual transcends the natural. Though men die, principles live.

The principles of the religion of Jesus, incorporated into His Church, and faithfully guarded, are imperishable.

"The words that I speak unto you, they are spirit, and they are life."

"Heaven and earth shall pass away, but my words shall not pass away."

A Church will fulfill its mission in the world only so long as it embodies the truth as it is in Jesus. "He that abideth in me, and I in him, the same bringeth forth much fruit: for without me ye can do nothing."

We rejoice with you, brethren, in your continuous prosperity. The present speaks for the past. Yonder tree stands burdened with foliage and fruit, because each successive year of its life, its leaves unfolding from deepest rootlet to topmost branch added strength to the tree. The present state of this venerable mother of churches reflects credit upon the names of the fathers who are dead as well as upon her living members.

"Their works do follow them," and their mantles have fallen upon others no less worthy. We rejoice that this day we can claim consanguinity with you, though our relationship be distant. But we count ourselves as a church particularly happy in the affiliation of neighborhood and family ties. The honored names mentioned in your history to-day are names familiar to us, and they remind us with pleasure that we are vitally connected with the social fabric which adorns this community.

May those strong natural ties grow firmer with years, and be held doubly sacred through the sanctifying grace of our common Redeemer. Men shall then say with pride : Behold how good and how pleasant it is for brethren to dwell together in unity ;" and even this shall remain a witness to the power of the religion of Jesus Christ.

We congratulate you on this, one of the proudest days of your existence, for your honored past, for your delightful present, and for your auspicious future, and may the wide streams of influence which go out from you this day become deepened and extended by the indwelling spirit of God, until time shall be no more.

LETTER FROM   -   WARREN RANDOLPH, D.D.

Licentiate and Pastor of the Central Baptist Church, Newport, R. I.

NEWPORT, June 11th, 1889.

TO THE PASTOR AND MEMBERS OF THE DEAR OLD MOTHER CHURCH, TO WHOM UNDER GOD I OWE MY SPIRITUAL LIFE AND MY CHRISTIAN INHERITANCE. BELOVED IN THE LORD:

Glad as I am to go upon the mission to which I have been appointed, I should have been specially glad if my departure could have been delayed long enough for me to have enjoyed the festivities in which you are to be engaged on the 20th instant. But time and tide—and ocean steamships—wait for no man. Brethren of various names, with whom I have long been associated, have requested me to represent them in the World's Sunday-school Convention, soon to meet in London, and that is the only reason of my absence from the rare occasion which will call you together.

A church-life of two hundred years, along what marvels in the world's history has it run parallel ! Coming into existence in the colonial times, this Church when nearly a hundred years old, saw the rise of the American Republic—saw it endure a tremendous strain—but, thank God, did not see it fall. It has seen slavery eliminated from the American Union, and the flag of freedom floating over its two and forty States.

In the last quarter of its history it has seen the greatest progress in Science, Art, Discovery and Invention which mankind have ever known. It has seen the rise also, and has itself been part of the great evangelizing agencies by which our own and other lands are being brought—slowly, to be sure, but most certainly—under the power of the Gospel.

With all the shocks and changes of the passing years it has held firmly to the principles in which it was established. Six generations of men have always found its light gleaming just where the fathers put it. Questions of a new Theology have not disturbed it, for it has always believed " the old is better." Singularly free from apostates and sensationalists in the pulpit, it has always had a virtuous and well instructed congregation in the pews. Beginning in 1689 with Thomas Killingsworth and John Drake, its first pastor, the Church has had, in the best sense, a royal line of preachers—men not ambitious of fame and popular applause, but given devoutly to their work. Of the living I may not speak—of the long since dead, I cannot, if I would. But upon the more recent graves of Daniel Dodge and Daniel D. Lewis and Henry V. Jones I would gladly lay laurel leaves to-day.

Father Dodge, to use his own expression, the last time I saw him, " dandled " me on his knee when I was an infant. I saw and heard him preach and pray and sing when I was a child. It comes to me now, as a glimpse of something almost seraphic, as this venerable man of God, with tears coursing down his cheeks, stood at the foot of the pulpit stairs and sung—

> " From whence doth this union arise,
>   That hatred is conquered by love ?
> It fastens our souls in such ties
>   As distance and time can't remove."

Father Lewis, who baptized me, ah how can we who had such a warm place in his heart, ever forget him ? The doctrines of grace how he gloried in them. And when, so soon after preaching on the Sabbath, it was announced that he " was not, for God took him," how sweet it was to think that the prayer we used to hear him so often offer was answered in his own experience, and that he was " in an actual and habitual readiness for the coming of the Son of Man."

At the mention of the name of Henry V. Jones—who married me and helped to ordain me—who of us does not even yet hear the music of the Gospel, as with soft and silvery voice he proclaimed it? If none of us ever heard him preach what are commonly called "great sermons," I doubt whether any of us ever heard him preach a poor one. If he never rose to great heights, he always had a most delightful level. His preaching was like the sweet pastures which the good shepherd is continually seeking out, and to which, day by day, he brings his flock. And "he being dead, yet speaketh."

Associated with these leaders of the host were devout and sympathizing helpers, without whom the Church could not have been what it has been. The leaders led so grandly, because they had followers who followed faithfully. Few churches have had more complete harmony between pastors and people—"to which the memory of man runneth not to the contrary."

Brethren, what a precious inheritance is yours. "Other men labored, and ye have entered into their labors." Hold up the banner of The Dear Old Church. May God give you grace to hold it firmly. In its place may it be kept till it is bathed in the light of millennial glory—till the Master, whom for two centuries it has honored, "shall appear the second time without sin unto salvation."

Your brother in Christ,

WARREN RANDOLPH.

ADDRESS BY - - - REV. C. J. PAGE.

Pastor of this Church from 1857 to 1867.

Whenever and wherever we meet a Church scripturally organized and "composed of living stones, built up a spiritual house to offer spiritual sacrifices acceptable to God by Jesus Christ," we feel like congratulating them. The knowledge we have of this people, having served them for years as pastor—meeting them under the varied circumstances in life, in sorrow and in joy—we know they are so organized, and so composed. "Built upon the foundation of the apostles and prophets, Jesus Christ Himself being the chief corner stone. In whom ye also are builded together for a habitation of God through the spirit." We congratulate you, because you have within yourselves the elements of power and expansion. It will be your own fault, if you do not attain to the perfect stature in Christ Jesus. Two hundred years, and what hath God wrought. Two hundred years ago a vine was brought out of the east, room was prepared for it, and it took deep root, and it filled the lands; the boughs thereof were like the goodly cedars. Under it men, women and children sat, and its fruit was

sweet to their taste. The boar out of the wood hath not wasted it,
nor hath the wild beast of the field devoured it. It is to-day an ever-
green like a "tree planted by the rivers of water." Other churches
have gone out from it, and the daughters and grand daughters are present to-day, and gathering round her, call her blessed. In the history
so faithfully sketched by Dr. Brown, we see the little one a thousand,
and the small one a strong people. I am thinking to-day of the
Runyons, Stelles, Dunns, Smiths, Drakes, Walkers, Daytons, Lupardus',
Smalleys, Randolphs—all of them were here when I served the
Church. Noble men and women, devoted to God, and loyal to the
truth, the Aarons and the Hurrs. What wise counsellors I had in
Jeremiah Stelle, Daniel Runyon, Alexander Dunn, Henry Smalley,
Samuel Smith, and others. Was ever pastor so blessed. They have
ceased from labor, and have entered into rest. But we hold them in
grateful remembrance. In looking over the audience, I am reminded
of the passage, "Instead of the fathers shall be the children." You
have come into their places, and have a goodly heritage. See to it
that you transmit it unimpaired to those who shall come after you.
The fathers of the Church, while so devoted to all its interests, had a
vein of quiet humor in them, and loved to perpetrate a joke even if
the pastor was laughed at. While I served them a farm was connected
with their parsonage, and as I began to stock it, Henry Lupardus in-
formed me that Samuel Dayton had a cow which he would sell, and
took me up to see it. After an examination I enquired the price, and
when told, said, well, I will take her; you may drive her down.
Evidently the two had exchanged glances, and Brother Dayton said:
Dominie I don't want to take the advantage of you on that cow. I
inquired what is the matter with her. Does she kick? No! Does
she jump fences? No! Give a good lot of milk? Yes! Make good
butter? None better in the township. Well, said I, what the plague
is the matter with her, and he replied : Well, to be honest with you,
she has no front teeth in her upper jaw. Well, said I, with uplifted
hands, I don't want her. Oh! how they laughed, and continued their
laughter until they saw I was displeased, and then said, why have you
lived so long and never knew that no cow has teeth there. It soon
spread through the parish, and even now your children sometimes
ask me, Dominie, how about that cow?

> "A little nonsense now and then
> Is relished by the best of men."

During my pastorate the rebellion was inaugurated, the great body
of the people would have rejoiced to escape the conflict. They prayed
against it, reasoned against it ; but it came, and the boys in blue were
equal to the occasion. The Township was required to furnish. 110
men. Dreading a draft, I was earnestly requested to take the command of the company, and consented to do so, but afterwards was
appointed Chaplain to the Regiment, Joseph C. Letson succeeding to
he Captaincy, and William H. Stelle, First Lieutenant. We formed
a part of the Twenty-eighth Regiment New Jersey Volunteers. The

following members of the Church were enrolled: Bro. Brantingham, Boice, Smith, J. N. Stelle, I. R. Stelle, W. H. Stelle, Jeremiah Dunn, and Benjamin Dudling. The first three mentioned are no more. Brothers Brantingham and Boice perished on the field of Fredericksburgh, while Bro. Smith, wounded in the same battle, fell a victim to that scourge of the soldier—typhoid fever. Of the congregation there went out from us, P. F. Runyon, J. Langstaff, W. McCrea, W. Merrill, J. C. Letson, S. R. Dayton, Calvin Drake, I. Dayton, W. Davis, R. Conway, A. Hummer and Geo. Stelle. The first four mentioned sealed their devotion to the country with their lives. Calvin Drake, I. R. Stelle, G. Stelle, J. C. Letson, bear honorable scars received in battle. The following who laid down their lives on the altar of their country represented other congregations. Field, Green, Toupet, Ryno, Lane, and Baker. 'Tis sad to contemplate their end. The monument erected to the memory of those who in defence of their country fell, has a purpose, and that purpose gives it character, that purpose enrobes it with dignity and moral grandeur. Its speech will be of patriotism and courage; of civil and religious liberty; of free government; of the moral improvement and elevation of mankind, and of the immortal memory of those who, with heroic devotion have sacrificed their lives for their country. It will also show that as there were no loyalists or tories among the fathers in the struggle for independence, so among their sons there were no secessionists.

Address by • • • REV. M. V. McDUFFIE,

Pastor of the Remsen Avenue Baptist Church of New Brunswick.

BRO. CHAIRMAN, BRETHREN AND SISTERS :

After listening to the very inspiring history of the Stelton Church, the Remsen Avenue Church, which has the honor to be one of the descendants along with the other daughters and grand-daughters present here to-day, rejoices with thankfulness to God for the peace, harmony and prosperity which characterized this venerable church through the two hundred years of its existence. And it may be that there is on the part of the daughters and grand-daughters present a little pardonable pride. Is it true, sir, that there is as much in the blood of folks as in the blood of horses? and as much in the blood of churches as in the blood of folks? If so, the members of this large family of churches represented here to-day have great responsibilities to consider; for there is much royal blood in their veins. The mother church has been the acknowledged queen of churches for two hundred years and still retains her position in our affections, and bears her honors gracefully, becomingly, humbly. But what is still more grati-

fying and pleasing to the children of the family is the fact that the old
mother shows no signs of the infirmities of age. She is still young and
vigorous, her eye is not dim neither is her natural force abated. Virtue is its own reward as we see in the cheerful and happy spirit and
quick discerning mind of those who have acted well their part in life's
conflicts. I bring to the church the hearty greetings of the Remsen
Avenue Church. This church came out of the First Church of New
Brunswick and is therefore a grand-daughter. Since 1872, at which
time we set up our banner in the name of God as an independent organization, we have received into our fellowship over 600 members.
Letters of dismission have been granted to 119 members to unite with
sister churches, others have been dismissed and excluded, while yet
others have died. The present membership of the church is 387.
Our Sunday School has nearly four hundred members on its roll, and
the largest average attendance of any Baptist school in our city. The
contributions of the church to objects of benevolence have been liberal
and the present condition is more than encouraging, it is even inspiring, as the growing condition of the congregation makes it necessary
for us to consider plans for the enlargement of our church building or
the erection of a new church.

Mention has been made of noble men whose labors under God
resulted well for the Stelton Church and the Baptist cause in this section, the saintly women have also made a record though many of their
names have been forgotten and left out of history. For Remsen Avenue Church I would say that much of the success of the church under
God, has been due to our consecrated women. In fact it was in the
heart of one of the mothers in Israel that the conception was first
formed of an organization which contributed liberally toward the
building of our present house of worship. In 1868, Mrs. Wm. Kent,
wife of Deacon Kent of the First Church, suggested the organization
of a Ladies' Aid Society for the purpose of raising money to assist in
building a new church. When the time came some money was ready
for the organization. That society led to the organization of an Aid
Society in the new church, which still exists. For many years it had
as its efficient secretary Miss Emma Stelle, a daughter of another deacon of the First Church. The women of our Baptist churches deserve
to be remembered in connection with the success of our churches.
We hope the venerable church whose bi-centennial we to-day celebrate
may have 200 more years of prosperity and peace added to its history.

Poem by - - - REV. C. C. SMITH.

Licentiate and Pastor of Baptist Church at Hempstead, L. I.

When we stand and behold from some eminence high,
The forest and meadow and streamlet and sky ;
When we see far away in the distances dim,
And nature is voicing her joy in a hymn;
We may seem to have gathered in beautiful view,
As in a fair picture the old and the new,
In which the rich blending of sunshine and shade,
Of the old and the new, the picture hath made :
And so from the mount of this year of our Lord,
The scenes in our thought fair pictures afford :
We look far away o'er the landscape of years,
The years of the past full of joys and of tears ;
We look all around, and we look on before,
And we look far beyond, to the years evermore :
And we gather in vision a picture so rare,
That it seems to the eye surpassingly fair :
The past in the distance is brought to our sight,
And it blends with the present as shadow with light ;
And the vision so rare of the time yet to be,
Melts away into thoughts of the bright crystal sea.

'Twas two centuries ago when a small Christian band,
Unfurled here their banner, and here took their stand ;
Here built they their fortress and stood for defence,
Of the truth as they held it in old Baptist sense ;
So they laid the foundations right strong and secure ;
They intended that fortress to stand and endure.
Since then, generations have followed each other,
And father, and mother, and sister, and brother,
Have lived out their day, and fallen on sleep :
Their vigils, the angels, o'er their ashes doth keep ;
In the great Judgment-day what they sowed they shall reap.
From that small beginning, two centuries span,
Not far from the banks of the old Raritan,
Those six earnest souls have increased by the score ;—
Full many are safe on the heavenly shore.
'Twas the fruitful seed that produces its kind,
When the seed that we sow in the harvest we find:
So out of the grain of this harvest-field,
God's reapers have gathered a bountiful yield:
Himself watched the planting of that tiny seed ;
Himself planned the work, and He blessed the deed.

It was not then as now,—sometimes courting disaster,—
That they searched all the country around for a pastor ;
But one of the six, whom they knew would they take ;
Their chosen was with them and they called Brother Drake.
For fifty long years he guarded the flock,
And like Moses of old who once smote the rock,
Though he saw not a burning bush yet unconsumed,
God's favor and kindness his pathway illumed.
It was not then the fashion for some leading brother,
To drive off the Pastor, then pray for another ;

But earnestly seeking to learn the good way,
They welcomed their Pastor's half century stay.
And so with the flock, where his first works were blended,
He lived and he worked, till his labors were ended.
'Twas prophetic of good for a plant very new,
And destined to flourish two centuries through,
To enjoy many years, to nurture and tend,
This Spiritual Gardener, the good Lord did send ;
And now, this old tree, that hath lasted so long,
Is laden with fruit, and is thrifty and strong.

Next came Brother Stelle, of Huguenot birth ;
A Magistrate, Preacher, and Pastor, of worth ;
And in place of the father, when his work was done,
Abundant in labors, came Isaac the son.
And the next Reune Runyon who thought it no harm,
While he tended the flock, to have also a farm.
Then, the good James McLaughlin, so earnest and grave,
By the word of the truth, sought the people to save.
After him Daniel Dodge ; that his work was much blest,
The souls won to Christ will quite surely attest.
Then came Daniel Lewis, a man true and plain ;
And one who took snuff, had a white-headed cane ;
Whose laugh was contagious, whose house was in town ;
The good people went for him, and they took him down ;
A reaper of harvest he gathered the sheaves,
And he gained the reward the good servant receives.
Then came Henry V. Jones, to Welshmen akin,
Who loved the pure gospel, and the people loved him :
His work was a blessing ; his word was in love ;
His memory is fragrant ; his reward is above.

After him, Christian Page, one quite rotund and strong,
And a man of the people who still battles the wrong ;
And many a soul to the gospel attent,
Gave heed to the word, and was brought to repent.
In the line of succession came scholarly Brown ;
A competent preacher for country or town ;
Expounding the word and preaching good news,
While the echo of pulpit, came back from the pews.
These two undershepherds,—and glad that they may,—
Are enjoying with us Bi-centennial day.
And still there's another, who yet in his zeal,
Recommends the Physician who only can heal ;
A man of the Lord, who is going about,
The pure sweet gospel preaching in season and out ;
And to-day he rejoices that of Pastors eleven,
He now shepherds a flock that is so much like Heaven.
Among all these good names we have Drake, Stelle and Runyon ;
There's McLaughlin, and Dodge, but never a Bunyan ;
And there's Lewis, and Page, and there's Brown, Sarles, and Jones ; —
These are all pleasing names of euphonious tones ;
Names all, you'll observe of moment and pith ;
But among them all there's not even a Smith.

But the names ! so familiar in dear old Piscataway !
And while you perchance muse o'er them and chat away,

How they come like old friends e'en to ask recognition !
And passing before you how they seem like a vision !
The Randolphs, and Daytons, the Drakes, and the Stelles ;
The Runyons and Letsons, and memory tells,
Of the Smiths and the Smalleys, the Hummers and Dunns ;
Of Mannings and Martins, and such other ones,
As Dunham and Dunbar and Benward and France,
And perhaps you might lengthen the long list perchance,
With Lupardus and Sutton and Conway and Mundy—
How many in meeting there were of a Sunday !
'Twas a sight, aye indeed ! on a fine Sunday morn,
To behold the full carriages rounding " Cape Horn !"
From the way to New Durham and the old Friendship road,—
Perhaps they'd have six or more in a load ;—
From Piscataway-town and the turnpike abode,
All wending their way to the house of God.
And what if the red mud adhered to the wheels,
Detaining them often quite late from their meals?
It still mattered not, they would be in their pew ;
They must hear what the Lord would have them to do.

These knights of the soil have been men of true worth,
Men of sense and religion, yet not without mirth ;
Nor averse yet to eating, a good turkey dinner :
And the saint would enjoy it as well as the sinner :
In the Summer they'd toil in the sweat of their face ;
In the Winter they'd visit and talk of their place ;
And if with the husband, wife and children went too,
It was thought quite the proper thing for them to do,
'Twas a neighborly way that they had with each other,
When neighbor to neighbor seemed almost a brother.
And the young people too, not averse to be friends,
With the mutual ease which youth kindly lends,
Would sometimes continue the friendship begun,
Till it budded and blossomed so under the sun,
That the only thing proper there was to be done.
Was for two molten hearts to blend into one. .
And so generations have passed with the years ;
Have passed with their trials, their joys, and their fears ;
These men of the soil have planted their fields,
And have gathered the harvests good husbandry yields ;
They have patiently waited for sunshine and rain ;
They have watched the returns of the seasons again :
In the hard working time they have toiled with their might,
And have laid themselves down to the sweet rest of night :
They have nurtured their children with parental care ;
They have reared men and women of excellence rare :
So on through the years son succeeded the sire,
Fulfilling in measure parental desire ;
And the children have reaped what the parents have sown,
In houses and substance and high moral tone.

And on these rural homes, what sweet rich benedictions,
Have descended in joy, as well as afflictions!
In the joy of the bridal ; in joy at the birth ;
In the joy of childhood's sweet innocent mirth ;
In the happy contentment of family love ;
At the altar of prayer as they looked up above :

Alas ! out from these homes where once they sojourned,
Have gone the beloved and have not returned !
How the walls of these houses full many a story,
Could relate of the saints thence gone home to glory ;
Of the Christian content and the soul full of peace,
As the Lord in His kindness gave to them release ;
As they plumed their wings, and in triumph took flight,
How they left in their track a pathway of light ;
As though they would lure up the heavenly way,
Those lingering yet in mortality's clay.

And what of the heroes, *our own* " boys in blue,"
Who died for the Union, for me and for you ?
Go and read on yon shaft, the fair names we engrave,
And think of the country *our* boys helped to save :
Let the names there inscribed be inscribed on our hearts ;
Let their memory be cherished, till memory departs.

'Tis a goodly assembly we are seeing to-night,
Of the children of those who have stood for the right ;
Who are noble successors of men true as steel ;
Men with heads that could think and with hearts that could feel.
All hail to the youths and the maidens, a band,
Who are serving the Lord with heart tongue and hand !
And we give them a welcome, and Christian salute ;
They have come the great army of God to recruit :
As the veterans fall one by one in the race,
It is well they are here thus to fill up the place.

And oh maidens ! forget not, if roses in pairs,
Like those worn by your mothers when bright youth was theirs,
Bloom now on YOUR cheeks as if kissed by the dew !
Oh forget not your mothers have shared theirs with you !
If instead of the dimples once seen on her face,
The deep lines of care have now taken their place ;
Remember how Nature doth kindly transmute,
The blossoms of Summer into Autumn's ripe fruit :
If the dimples, sweet blossoms, were fair to behold,
Changed now into fruit, they are apples of gold.

And oh boys, of such princes, such fathers as thine !
If in you all their manhood and virtues combine;
Oh remember that fathers live life o'er again,
In the lives of their sons as they grow to be men :
As their own strength declines in yours they'll be strong ;
And your virtues and manhood to them will belong.

Though the past has its annals and this day its cheer,
What lies in the future doth not wholly appear :
But we're treading the pathway which leads up the height ;
We have reached each a lookout, and oh ! what a sight !
At the top of the mount is the cloud that conceals,
The glorious vision faith only reveals ;
But into that cloud that concealeth God's face,
The footsteps of glorified spirits we trace :

And lo, others are passing on up out of sight,
And out of earth's darkness on into God's light !
As we look down the mountain on those coming after.
There are sighs, there are tears, there is joy, there is laughter ;
But mingling along with that laboring train,
We behold on the steep and out over the plain,
The Elect, the Lord's Chosen ; —He knoweth His own ;
He is guiding their footsteps safe up to His throne.

And shall *we* too ascending this mountain of Time,
Attain to the heights of the glory sublime ?
And into that cloud that concealeth God's face,
Shall we follow the spirits whose footsteps we trace ?
This mountain enshrouded shall not always stay ;
For the Scriptures declare, Time shall vanish away.

ADDRESS BY   -   -   -   REV. WM. ROLLINSON.

Pastor of the Rahway Baptist Church.

BRETHREN AND FRIENDS :

From the programme you learn that as one of the senior pastors
I am desired to speak a few congratulatory words at the closing up of
these delightful services, but I prefer to base my privilege on the right
of kinship rather than on that of seniority. My good friend, Dr.
Parmly (we were boys together) suggested that I should forecast the
future, since so much has been said of the past of this honored Church,
but as I have not yet reached an age when

> " The sunset of life gives us mystical lore,
> And coming events cast their shadows before."

I will spare you any prophecies save those uttered by the voices of the
past, which clearly and loudly predict a prosperous future as the
natural outgrowth of a noble and devoted past.

I said I claim kinship with this Church. I do, and I will tell you
how and why, for the kind of relationship I claim has been urged by
no other to-day—I am a great-grandchild of Piscataway Church.

We have heard much and very pleasantly, both morning and
afternoon, of the family connections of this ancient Church. Her
children, all of whom are themselves venerable for age, and her grandchildren, each one of whom has attained to full spiritual stature, have
come up to the bi-centennial feast prepared by the mother Church,
and as one after another they have spoken to us, through their respective pastors, so numerous has been the spiritual progeny that as we
have listened to their loving words and their filial greetings, we might
be excused for feeling that it would not be strange were most of those

present to search out their genealogys if they should say of Piscataway Church what Paul said of the Jerusalem from above,—"She is the mother of us all." In my ministerial capacity I myself, am a great-grandchild, as it was the First Baptist Church of New York City, a child of the Scotch Plains Church, itself the oldest daughter of this Church, which called me into the gospel ministry, and were this all I would rightly feel myself one of the family. But many other things fit me to rejoice with the brethren here and with their loved pastor. For the whole period of my ministerial life I have known and loved this Church ; during twenty-seven years of my pastoral life it has been, as it is now, the Baptist Church nearest in one direction, to the one I have served, and every pastor it has had for the last fifty years, I have personally known and esteemed, while with the present pastor my relations have been peculiarly intimate and interesting. In youth we were converted under the same ministry ; were baptized in the same pool; belonged to the same church, taught in the same Sunday-School and sat together under the ministry of that Prince in Israel, Spencer H. Cone ; and since then we have stood together, holding fast to the form of sound words received from those honored lips, contending for the same principles, defending the same truths and preaching the same old gospel, so that personal reasons, in addition to the interest belonging to the occasion which has drawn us here, make me glad to participate in the joy of this pastor's heart and to join in the hearty congratulations offered to him and to the church he so loyally and lovingly serves, on an event which but once before, on this Continent at least, has occurred in the history of our denomination—the bi-centennial of a Baptist Church.

In the deeply interesting historical paper prepared and read by Dr. Brown, we have been shown something of the meaning of a bi-centennial anniversary, and it has come to my mind with almost startling force that the period of church life enjoyed by this Church covers more than one-tenth of the entire Christian era. Ten such periods would take us back to a time a hundred years and more before the angels sang the first gospel hymn on the hills of Bethlehem, or the magi followed the star which led them to the manger-cradle of the Son of God.

Led by the vivid descriptions of the accomplished historian of this Church, we have lived in fancy through two centuries of the buried past, and have shared, sympathetically, in the toils, struggles and sacrifices of the noble men and women who were the pioneers of our Baptist faith, as they opened the path for Christ's truth to advance— only a woodman's trail at first, but steadily broadening as they toiled, till it has become like the King's highway, with a score and more of churches like their own in faith and practice gracing its borders ; and in thus living over again the years of past faith and heroism, we have learned the significance of this bi-centennial occasion, and have felt how fitting it was for the old mother to call us to rejoice with her on the completion of the two hundredth year of her life, ere she again sets her face towards the future still "strong in the Lord and in the power of his might," feeling as did Paul at Appii forum, when the brethren came to meet him, "whom, when he saw, he thanked God and took courage."

I have spoken of this as an old church, but we have felt the pulse of its bounding life to-day, and as we look on the gay and costly attire in which the aged mother is arrayed for her birthday festival, she seems to have found what Ponce de Leon vainly sought—the fountain of rejuvenescence. But how can she ever feel the palsy of age who draws her life from the great lifegiver? After two hundred years we find the old church as Moses was in his age, with eye undimmed and vigor unabated ; still she sees the truth as the father's saw it, and grown but the stronger because of her years, she keeps in the van of her offspring no one of whom will she suffer to excel her in zeal and devotion to God's truth and Christ's honor. All this we have seen to-day, and I am sure I express no more than the universal feeling, when I say of the Piscataway Church, that it has been to this entire region like a spring of living waters, forth from which have flowed streams which have made spiritual deserts blossom as the rose, and that her past centuries are the sufficient pledge of her power and potency in future ones. And I think of no more fitting words to speak in closing than those it will be the rapture of the redeemed to hear when spoken by the Master's lips : *"Well done! good and faithful servant."*

The following letters were read during the day.

TRENTON, N. J., June 1, 1889.

MY DEAR DR. SARLES:

It would be a great pleasure for me to be present at the Bi-Centennary Anniversary of the Church and to meet with so many of the families endeared to me by professional relations and by personal friendship. I have always been glad that I was born in Piscataway Township, and that my maternal ancestor Griffith, who is buried so close to the meeting house was a Baptist deacon. Although absent I shall thank God and rejoice with you in all the blessings and precious memories of the past, and anticipate still greater prosperity and grace for the future. With kindest regards to all,

I beg to remain,

EZRA M. HUNT.

PHILADELPHIA, June 20, 1889.

Too weak to meet with you in person to-day. We send our cordial greeting.   C. L. LEE,

C. P. FARSON.

OUTLINE SKETCHES

—OF THE—

PIONEER PROGENITORS OF THE PISCATAWAY PLANTERS

1666- 1716.

BY OLIVER B. LEONARD, ESQ.

PLAINFIELD, N. J.

THE names of the first pioneers to settle on the Raritan were Hugh Dunn, John Martin, Hopewell Hull and Charles Gillman, with their families. On the 21st of May, 1666, they were granted the right as associates of the Woodbridge patentees, and December 18, following, were deeded by these New England neighbors from Newbury, one-third of their purchase obtained the week before. During the next year there came other members of the Gillman and Hull families, also Robert Dennis and John Smith. So cheerful were the prospects and complete the liberties established; so peaceful the plantation and so generous the inducements offered, that additional emigration soon followed by friends and neighbors of the original pioneers. Before the year 1670 passed, the settlement of Piscataway had been increased by many new arrivals of associate planters from New England. Among them were Francis Drake, Benajah Dunham, Henry Langstaff and John Martin, with their families, from New Hampshire; John Fitz-Randolph, with his brothers, Thomas, Joseph and Benjamin, and sisters Elizabeth and Ruth, with their parents; Geoffry Manning, Nicholas Bonham, Samuel Walker and John Smalley, with their wives and children, from other New England districts, where the intolerance of the established Church order had restricted and restrained the exercise of free conscience and subjected them to many indignities and deprivations.

But the required number of actual settlers had not yet purchased land in Piscataway and made such improvements as were contemplated and specified by the Woodbridge grant of 1666, and the previous charter of 1664 to the Elizabethtown colony. Four years had now intervened without realizing the necessary accessions to the population or the required development of the territory. On the 20th of October, 1670, Governor Carteret made a public proclamation waiving all objections that might be made against the Piscataway settlement "on account of their not having come in exactly according to the time limited." Stimulated by this official concession, renewed efforts were immediately made resulting in the greater improvement of the country and an increase of emigration thither. By 1675-6 Piscataway had attained a notable prominence in the civil affairs of the province, and that year sent for the first time two deputies to the General Assembly, which had been held but twice before, (during the

Spring and Winter of 1668) The few accessions made during the five years succeeding—1676-81—may have been caused by the disputed title of boundaries between
Piscataway and Woodbridge, and the division of ownership in the colony and the
unsettled condition of proprietorship, which was not definitely determined till 1682.

QUAKER GOVERNMENT.

At this date additional impetus was imparted to emigration thither. William
Penn, at the head of a real estate syndicate of Friends, purchased all of the unoccupied land of East Jersey at an auction sale in London, on the 2d of February, 1682.
These Quaker proprietors were not slow in making known in England and Scotland
the remarkable advantages of this new country. They gave reassurance that the
liberal terms of the Constitution formerly granted, would be assiduously maintained;
as well as the unrestricted rights of all settlers in matters of religion.

By this time—1682-'89, the date of the organization of the Piscataway Baptist
Church—the limits of the township had been enlarged, and fully eighty families were
occupying the territory. The following names are then found among the prominent
freeholders as recently arrived citizens, whose religious affiliations were with the Baptist people : Vincent Runyon, Nicholas Mundy, James Giles, Andrew Wooden, and
representatives of the Suttons, Holtons, Daytons, Mollisons, and others. Up to this
period nearly all the planters had come from plantations in New England or Long
Island, and been under the influence of instruction tending to Baptist doctrines.
Most all of the first original settlers in Piscataway were imbued with religious principles of this denomination, which had been discernable among the earliest adventurers
to New England, and been preached by Hanserd Knollys in New Hampshire and
taught by Roger Williams in Massachusetts and Rhode Island, and advocated by
William Wickenden among the towns on Long Island.

By the time the government of East Jersey passed into the hands of the Crown
—1702, and a few years thereafter at the distribution of the back lands—local history
of Piscataway becomes familiar with the names of the Stelles, Blackfords, Clarksons,
Piatts, Coriells, Brokaws, Boices, Bishops, Fords, Merrells, Higgins, Hendricks,
Slaters, Fields, Laings, Websters, Pounds, Clarks, Thorns, Lupardus's and others.

THE DUNNS AND DUNHAMS,

with the Drakes, shortly after them, came to this township from the Piscataqua
district in New England.

Hugh Dunn, the founder of this family name in New Jersey, was devoutly
religious, and encouraged the early settlers by exhorting them to a holy living. His
advocacy of an untrammeled conscience in the worship of God, greatly aided in the
enjoyment of the Gospel in purity and peace. He lived through all the trying times
of establishing a new colony, and died in 1694. This was five years after the public
organization of the Baptist Church, of which he was a constituent member, and for
the realization of which he toiled and prayed. His descendants have always been
prominent members in the faith of their mother Church, and that of the sister branch
observing the seventh day as their Sabbath.

The Dunhams, of Piscataway, (for there was a different lineage of same name at
Woodbridge), had as their progenitor a worthy sire in the person of Benajah Dunham. Their family tradition asserts that he settled in this vicinity several years
previous to its formal occupation by any other Englishmen. His first child born was
Edmund, whose birth in 1661 was the earliest of any white child born in the township. Edmund Dunham grew to be an influential member of society, and became a
lay preacher, helping to mould the tender consciences and direct the religiously in-
clined of the pioneer community. In 1681 he married Mary, or Elizabeth Bonham, a
member of another early planter's family. Their son, Jonathan, in after years,
succeeded his father in the ministry of the Seventh-Day Baptist Church, of Piscataway,
of which the father may be said to be the founder in 1705-7.

THE DRAKES.

The Drakes of this part of New Jersey are the direct descendants of Francis and
Mary Drake, who moved into this township about 1667-8 from the New Hampshire
district of same name. The ancestors of Francis Drake had lived there on the banks

of the swift-flowing Piscataqua River since 1635. Among the first of this name to settle in the new world in that New England locality was Robert Drake, a man of eminent piety. At his death in 1667 two or three sons survived him—Nathaniel, Abraham and probably Francis, the progenitor of the New Jersey line. By some it is claimed that Francis, last named, was the grandson of Sir Francis Drake's brother Thomas, to whom the Admiral left his valuable estate, by others he is believed to have been his nephew. Robert Drake, first mentioned, was co-temporary with Sir Francis, his birth occurring in 1580, the same year the great navigator sailed around the world, in honor of which marvellous circuit of the globe at the age of thirty years, Queen Eliza-beth knighted him. Both Robert and Sir Francis belonged to the original family of Devonshire, Eng., where the Drake estate was established shortly after the conquest of William of Normandy.

In 1556 there was a Robert Drake living, who suffered as a martyr-minister in a neighboring county for conscience's sake, and was burned at the stake April 23 of that year. It is recorded of him that he said, when exhorted by the priest to renounce his faith: "As for your Church of Rome, I utterly deny its works and defy its power, even as I deny the devil and defy all his works."

FRANCIS DRAKE, who was the founder or the family in New Jersey, was a peti-tioner in 1665 at Dover, N. H, for protection to his property and religious rights. But the province being settled entirely as a trading interest, all laws were disregarded and a permanent residence there by peaceful citizens became unendurable. This same year the liberal concessions by the East Jersey proprietors were proclaimed in that region and Francis Drake, with others, shortly afterwards availed themselves of the generous invitation and moved to these quiet fields, where he spent the rest of his life till 1687, the year of his death. His sons Francis, George and John, born in New England, came with him, and their posterity has materially assisted in peopling this province for generations past. Of George, it is known that he married, in 1677, Mary Oliver, of Elizabethtown, and was a useful public servant of the township and colony. He was appointed supervisor of many important local matters and served as a legislator in the General Assembly for 1684 and several successive years following. From his sons George and Andrew many useful and industrious citizens have descended who helped to make the Church and community an honor and a blessing. The Rev. George Drake and Simeon J Drake were descendants of this line.

JOHN DRAKE, the most distinguished son of Francis, became a lay preacher in the early days of the settlement, and in after years, as is generally known, was the regular pastor of this Church. He married, in 1677, Rebecca Trotter, his first wife, daughter of one of the original associates of Elizabethtown, who came from Newbury, Mass. Pastor Drake had, by this and two other marriages, thirteen children, whose names are recorded as John, Francis, Samuel, Joseph, Benjamin, Abraham, Sarah, Isaac, Rebecca, Jacob, Ebenezer and Ephraim. These and the children of George and Francis Drake have left numerous and worthy descendants whose many virtues of mind and heart have always endeared the name to this and every locality where they have taken up a home. Time will not permit even an allusion to the honorable and eminent positions of usefulness attained by them in the different professions, and the progress made in the arts and sciences through the influence of those who have borne the name.

THE GILLMANS.

The Gillmans of New Jersey are descendants of John and Charles Gillman, two of the original patentees of Piscataway plantation in 1666-8. They came from the Piscataqua district of New Hampshire, where their ancestor, Edward Gillman, of Norfolk County, England, had settled shortly after his landing in 1638, in Massa-chusetts. The father had been a near neighbor of godly old John Robinson, of dis-senting notoriety before separating from the Church of England, and was heartily in sympathy with non-conformists.

THE HULLS AND LANGSTAFFS

came to Piscataway from the district in New Hampshire of the same name. In the pioneer days of that early New England settlement Benjamin Hull was a preacher of the gospel there. Whether he is the same person as the Piscataway patentees of that name who settled on the Raritan, the writer cannot say. From the earliest colonizations in New England the name has been prominent among the intelligent and outspoken freemen of the New World. A full generation before any of the family moved to New Jersey, Rev. Joseph Hull is mentioned as an original patentee of the town of Barnstable, Mass., where the Fitz-Randolphs, Bonhams, Smiths, and other Piscataway settlers came from. The pastor of the old First Baptist Church, of Boston, in 1675, was Rev. Isaac Hull, the same church whose meeting house doors were nailed up in 1680 by order of the Court of that colony. But few families can produce a longer list of remarkable ministers of the Gospel extending through colonial times to the present.

HOPEWELL and BENJAMIN HULL were the worthy founders of this family in New Jersey, which furnished in subsequent years some of the most influential personages of the local township government. In the peaceful pursuit of industry as well, their name is always found in honorable relations.

HENRY LANGSTAFF, the founder of the family in New Jersey, was the son of Henry, who emigrated to New Hampshire with the colony sent out by Mason, the patentee, in 1630. He lived on the Piscataqua River up to the time of his removal to Piscataway township in 1668-9. Through his son John, born in New England in 1647, the name has been handed down to posterity in this latitude. The marriage of many of the female members into other pioneer families, has given some of the best representatives of this mother Church. The original male line was distinctly identified with the Episcopal Church.

THE MARTINS.

Among the brave and bold passengers of the "Mayflower" was a representative of the MARTIN family, who sought "the wild New England shore for freedom to worship God." One of this familiar name was among the first planters to make a permanent settlement in this colony of conscience. John Martin, a Piscataway grantee of 1666, came here from the Piscataqua district in New Hampshire, where he lived as early as 1648 with the ancestors of the Dunns, Drakes, Langstaffs, and other old and respected families of that locality. The Martins came to stay, as a numerous line of descendants testify from that remote day to the present.

THE SMALLEYS

JOHN SMALLEY, of Plymouth, old England, came over to America in the vessel "Francis and James," 1632, with Edward Winslow and others. His native home was in the same shire of the Drakes, who had lived there from the days of the Norman conquest. Descendants of this name soon found a congenial place with the Baptists in Rhode Island. From that colony of liberty-loving people John Smalley came to Piscataway during its early infancy. His descendants have always held to the views of Christian truth as believed and practiced by the Baptists. The family gave to this denomination and trained in the doctrines by this Church, one of the most useful ministers of the gospel that ever labored in New Jersey—the Rev. Henry Smalley of blessed memory.

THE DENNIS'S.

ROBERT DENNIS, though a Piscataway patentee, lived in the adjoining settlement of Woodbridge, was descended from Thomas Dennis, an emigrant with Winthrop, who came to Massachusetts in 1630. The home of this pioneer before coming to New Jersey, was at Yarmouth, on Cape Cod, not far from the residence of other planters living in Barnstable. Several of the female members were united in marriage with the Fitz-Randolphs, Mannings, and others connected with the Baptists.

THE DAYTONS,

of New Jersey, are of New England origin, settling first in Massachusetts colony as early as 1637, and thence to Long Island. Their English ancestry occupied for a long time a homestead on the east bank of the Midway River, in Kent County. The settlement of this family in old Piscataway about the close of the pioneer days—1716-26—added a valuable element to the agricultural population. Some of their best representatives have had their names on the church roll of this and other neighboring Baptist churches.

THE CLARKSONS,

of East Jersey, trace their pedigree through Matthew Clarkson, who was Secretary of the province of New York from 1689 to his death, 1702. The founder of this American line was Rev. David Clarkson. of Bradford, York County, Eng. Many of this family were early identified with the Baptists by their marriage into families of the Stelles, Mannings, Randolphs, and others distinctly connected with this denomination. They removed from the province of New York into this township about the same time the Daytons' settlement here.

THE SUTTONS,

also, came from Long Island, descending from an honorable ancestry in the county of Nottingham, Eng., where the progenitor of Fitz-Randolphs lived before emigrating to this country. This family furnished to New Jersey many excellent Baptist preachers during the Colonial and Revolutionary times, one family had four distinguished sons in the ministry. Some of them were among the first to push into the interior to develop the Passaic valley and the hill country beyond, and at a later date moved to the western part of Pennsylvania.

THE WALKERS,

of Piscataway, were intimately associated with the religious interests of the Baptist denomination several years before the principles were crystalized into church form here. Samuel Walker, Isaac and Francis Walker, are early mentioned among the landholders of the township. Samuel was a prominent citizen in the province at the time of the constitution of this Church, and after the government of the Proprietors was surrendered to the Royal control, he became an influential member of Lord Cornbury's Council. The name has always furnished honorable and useful members in this and neighboring Baptist churches.

THE BONHAMS.

NICHOLAS BONHAM came to Piscataway from Barnstable, Mass , about 1669, being a neighbor there of the Fitz-Randolph family. He was married January 1, 1658, to Hannah Fuller, the oldest child of Samuel Fuller, one of the original passengers in the " Mayflower," and Jane Lothrop, daughter of the distinguished Puritan preacher. Their daughter, Mary, married Rev. Mr. Dunham in 1681, with whom his son, Hezekiah Bonham, about 1700, had the traditional conversation concerning secular labor on the Lord's day, which resulted in the ultimate establishment of the Seventh Day Society of Piscataway, in 1705-7, when its constituent members withdrew from the mother Church for that purpose.

THE FITZ-RANDOLPHS.

By far the most numerous representatives of any one family in the township were the Fitz-Randolphs, who descended from a distinguished Norman line settling in England with William the Conqueror, A. D. 1066. They became owners of vast estates in Yorkshire and the adjacent county of Nottingham. From the last named shire came EDWARD FITZ-RANDOLPH, the ancestor of the American family, who settled with his parents in Massachusetts about 1630, at the town of Scituate. In early manhood he married Elizabeth Blossom, of Puritan stock, and their children, born at Barnstable in the Plymouth colony, that lived to grow up and become heads of families, were Nathaniel, Hannah, Mary, John Joseph, Elizabeth, Thomas, Hope and Benjamin.

NATHANIEL FITZ-RANDOLPH, the oldest, born in 1642, became a Quaker, and one of the most influential of the sect. He migrated to Woodbridge township in 1678-9, locating near the Blazing Star ferry. He was the father of eight children, and a man of remarkable usefulness and importance in the commonwealth, filling all the local and county offices and prominent in the colonial government. His brothers, John, Joseph, Thomas and Benjamin, just mentioned, had moved to Piscataway ten years earlier – in 1668-9 — and were all of the Baptist persuasion except Benjamin. The emigration of this family to New Jersey was prompted by the severe enactments of the court of the old colonies, prohibiting the free exercise of individual consciences, compelling every person to sustain by tax the established Church worship, and imposing banishment upon any who opposed infant baptism.

JOHN FITZ-RANDOLPH, the oldest of the Piscataway branch, was born in 1653, and married Sarah Bonham in 1675. He is known as a constituent member of this Church and one of the largest landholders in the township.

JOSEPH FITZ-RANDOLPH, the next oldest, born in 1656, was father of twelve children by his wife, Hannah Conger, a member of one of the Woodbridge families. None of this familiar name attained to greater usefulness in the Church and colony than their immediate descendants. To verify the statement would only require the mention of the heirs of his son, Joseph, who married Rebecca Drake; and his daughter, Hannah, who married Andrew Drake ; and his son, Jonathan, whose wife was Margaret Manning; and his daughter, Prudence, who married Nathaniel Manning.

THOMAS FITZ RANDOLPH, the third son of the old patriarch, was born in 1659, and married Eliza Manning, having only six children. He was Clerk of the township and one of the first group of Selectmen to manage the affairs of the town, and served as deputy in the General Assembly.

BENJAMIN FITZ-RANDOLPH, the youngest, born 1663, married Sarah Dennis, and was taken in as a townsman of Piscataway in 1684 but moved to Princeton in 1696-9 with a colony of Friends whom William Penn induced to settle on a fertile plantation watered by Stony Brook, a tributary of the Millstone River.

These five Fitz Randolph brothers were progenitors of a numerous and prominent family-lineage who produced some of the best citizens of colonial days and give) to the State and country illustrious soldiers and statesmen, eminent legislators and jurists, learned professors, distinguished divines, successful merchants and valuable members of society in the more quiet walks of life.

THE MANNINGS.

The Manning surname is early found among the Saxons in the fifth century, from whence the family migrated to the counties of Kent, Sussex and Norfolk, in England. Within the first decade after the " Mayflower " landed her precious freight of human lives, the name is familiar in the Massachusetts colony at Boston and neighboring settlements. The founder of the family in New Jersey was Geoffery Manning, who, with his wife, Hephzibah, (daughter of Joseph Andrews, of Hingham, Mass.), settled in Piscataway about the time of the Fitz-Randolphs—1668-70. He was one of three commissioners to lay out the land grants in the township in 1682 and the following year was made an officer in the first County Court of Middlesex, held that year in Piscataway. His death is recorded in 1693. From his four sons, John, Joseph, James and Benjamin, came the numerous families of this name in East Jersey, especially in this and neighboring townships and the adjoining counties of Somerset and old Essex.

BENJAMIN MANNING married Ann Blackford, 1698.

JOHN MANNING, born 1670, married Elizabeth Dennis, 1693.

JOSEPH MANNING, married Temperance Fitz-Randolph.

JAMES MANNING, married Christiana Laing, and his immediate descendants became the most distinguished branch of the family during colonial times. From this last line came President Manning, of Brown University, a learned and eloquent minister of the Baptist denomination, and Jeremiah Manning, the fearless soldier of the Revolution, and Captain Nathaniel Manning, of eminent distinction in the earlier Indian wars.

From the beginning of pioneer settlements in East Jersey the Mannings have always been identified with the organization of the Baptist churches north of the Raritan. 'Among the first names on the record of this mother church some of the family are found. As the country developed and settlers moved inland the name is among the constituency of the Scotch Plains Church—and at the beginning o ⌐ the Samptown Church its first office-bearers were selected from the family. So at the organization of the Baptists in Plainfield and elsewhere, no more efficient and energetic members enlisted in the cause than were furnished by descendants of the original progenitor of this distinguished line.

HUGUENOTS.

In the list of the early Christians who made Piscataway Township their abiding place and became identified with the mother church should be mentioned a few families of French ancestry. These embrace the names of the Piatts, Boices, Lupardus',

Coriells and Brokaws, who early joined the colony of industrious Baptists. Their fore-fathers had endured hardships innumerable on account of religious beliefs in native France, and barbarous severities had been inflicted upon them because of their refusal to accept "the King's religion."

RUNYONS.

Among the multitude of Christian "exiles for conscience sake" from France was also the Huguenot family of the Runyons, transplanted to America about 1665. The founders of this large and influential line of pioneers, settled in East Jersey on the Elizabeth Town Grant as early as 1668-70. His name first appears as ' VINCENT RONGNION, mariner of Poitou." By modern orthography the family is now known as Runyon, with numerous representatives in every State of the Union. The district from which the progenitor of the the Runyons in America came was one that ex-perienced the most cruel desolation of property, and whose consecrated people en-dured more inhuman abuses than any other outraged province in the Empire. These devoted Protestants manifested the most unexampled heroism under sufferings, and yet proved steadfast adherents to their religious convictions.

The most popular and diabolical measure of the Papal authorities for intimidating these "obdurate heretics" and securing enforced conversions among them in this Province of Poitou, was the military occupation by the Dragonades quartered upon their families. This system of outrages impoverished the inhabitants, paralyzed all their industries and finally depopulated whole communities. For rather than bow the knee to Baal ; from this strong hold of Calvinism emigrated thousands of the faithful to Holland and England and other islands of the sea. From thence multitudes sought a refuge in this country for permanent homes. It is a reliable tradition that the founder of the Runyon family in America escaped from these cruel persecutions in his native place, to the Isle of Jersey, off the coast of France, and from there took ship to this country. The first reference to his name on this side of the waters is seen A. D. 1668, in a "marriage license" given by Philip Carteret, the young Governor of East Jersey. The document is on file in the office of Secretary of State of New Jersey, at Trenton, and reads as follows :

To any of the Justices of the Peace or Ministers of the Province of New Jersey :

Whereas. I have received information of a mutual agreement between Vincent Rongnion, of Portiers, in France, and Ann Boutcher, the daughter of John Boutcher, of Hartford, in England, to solemnize marriage together, for which they have re-quested my lycense, and there appearing no lawful impediment for the obstruction thereof, these are to require you or cyther of you, to joyne the said Vincent Rognion and Ann Boutcher in matrimony, and them to pronounce man and wife, and to make record thereof, according to the laws in that behalf provided, for the doing whereof this shall be to you or cyther of you a sufficient warrant.

Given under my hand and seal of the Province, the 28th of June, 1668, and the 20th year of the raigne of our Sovereign Lord Charles the Second, of England, Scot-land and Ireland, king, defender of the faith, &c.

(*Signed*)   *Ph. Carteret.*

This couple were joyned in matrimony by me the 17th of July, 1668.

(*Signed*)   *James Bolton.*

Ann Boutcher, the newly wedded wife of Vincent Runyon, may have been a descendant of the same family as Joan Boutcher, of Kent, a lady of distinction and piety, who was a Baptist and was burned at the stake May 2, 1550, within sight of the Canterbury Cathedral.

The next public notice of Vincent Runyon's name is found as owner of a piece of ground at Elizabeth Town, which he bought March 20, 1671-2. He was probably induced to make his first settlement at that place because of the national affinity of many of the early settlers. The Governor himself was of Norman French ancestry, and the Surveyor General, Robert Vanquellin, came from Caen, in France. The is *Hev.*

Secretary of the Province, James Bolton, was also of French extraction and besides there emigrated with Gov. Carteret a number of French men and women. Mr. Runyon did not remain long among that settlement, for the stern Puritan element predominated and rendered his relations unpleasant. Disposing of his town property as soon as possible the next public notice of him was in the Baptist community at Piscataway, where ever afterward he and his descendants have lived. Here on the Raritan River, in the spring of 1677, he purchased a farm of 154½ acres and from the homestead established there, went out the many children of this distinguished sire to become the founders of other large and influential lines of the Runyon family.

The sons and daughters of Vincent and Ann Boutcher Runyon were : Vincent, Darich, Joseph, Reune, Ephraim, Mary, Peter, Jane and Sarah, all born several years before the public organization of the Piscataway Baptist Church.

VINCENT, the oldest son, married Mary Hull 1691, and had children to the number of eleven : Sarah, Martha, Rezia, Mary, Anna, Vincent, Reuben, Reune, and three dying in infancy.

PETER, the youngest son, born 1680, married 1704, Providence Blackford, and had five sons and four daughters : John, Joseph, Peter, Richard, Benjamin, Grace, Rosannah, Providence and Sarah.

The other sons and daughters married into the families of Randolph, Sutton, Holton, Webster, Cooper, Layton, Bray, Mollison, Martin and Mannings, and many of their descendants are here to-day at the roll call of their forefathers.

STELLES.

To conclude the worthy list of those who through faith, experienced trials, endured persecutions and overcame all opposition for the truth sake, let grateful mention be made of such as bear the name of Stelle.

The progenitor of the Stelles in the United States was a Frenchman named Poncet Stelle (known among his descendants in America as Pontius Stelle). He was born about 1650, and was living at the time of his emigration to this country, about 1665, in the south-western part of France. His wife's name was Eugenie Legereau, a christian woman of earnest faith and devoted piety. Both were Protestants of the " reformed religion " designated in history since the Reformation of the 16th Century as " Huguenots," a name signifying decided and faithful adherence to Scriptural injunction—hence Bible christians, the recital of whose terrible struggles and sufferings for their religious belief, forms one of the most thrilling chapters in modern history.

From the records of the French Protestant Church in New York, of which he was a member, it is learned that Poncet Stelle came from Lorieres, France. A town of the same name at the present time is near the manufacturing city of Limoge. The locality is southerly from Poitiers, which was one of the strongest citadels of Huguenot faith, and in a region almost entirely occupied by devout christians of the Protestant religion just before the revocation of the Edict of Nantes. Disciples of the Reformation rapidly multiplied throughout the whole kingdom of France, but especially in the provinces situated between the rivers Loire and Garonne the doctrines of the new religion found ardent advocates in great numbers.

Poncet Stelle came from one of these provinces where the Reformers' followers were numerous. It was because the population of this portion of France was largely Protestant that the Papal authorities inflicted such direful persecution, and enforced such satanic schemes for their extermination or their acceptance of the doctrines of the Romish Church.

Among the Protestant exiles from France, by way of Holland, to settle in the vicinity of Hudson River was the founder of this family in America. It is a traditional statement that Poncet Stelle was one of the early French settlers on Staten Island, afterward removing to New York About 1660 a colony of Huguenots had located on the south-east side of Staten Island and were ministered to occasionally by the pastor of the French Protestant Church in the present City of New York. About the time that several Huguenot families removed from Staten Island and settled in the Hackensack Valley in 1678, others of their co-religionists moved to New York City, and among them " Sieur Poncet Stelle des Lorieres " as he is best known in public print. He was the sole progenitor of this family name in the United States.

unless others of his same lineage emigrated to this country under a different name. For example his sister Catherine was known by the name of the town she came from in France, viz : Catherine de Loriere, though she signed herself Catherine Stelle.

In the list of Baptisms performed during the early days of this French Church in New York City are the names of the children of Poncet Stelle, all of whom were born after 1680 and not later than 1695 : Benjamin, born, 1683 ; Gabriel, born 1685 ; Ambrose, born 1687 ; Madelaine, born 1689 ; Isaac, born 1690 ; John, born 1693, and possibly Eugene the last.

It would be interesting to trace the outline of Gabriel Stelle who became a large landholder in Monmouth County and a very wealthy man. He was a prominent member of St. Peter's Protestant Episcopal Church, of Amboy, in which city he died 1738, leaving a valuable estate to his wife Margaret.

No less interesting would it be to refer to the other Monmouth families of Ambrose, Isaac and John Stelle, all of whom were valuable citizens of that same rich county in the early days preceding the Revolution. But the Baptist denomination is indebted solely to BENJAMIN STELLE the oldest son and the founder of the Piscataway family, for the many steadfast christian examples of generations past and present bearing the Stelle name.

BENJAMIN STELLE was born in New York, A. D., 1683, and settled among the Piscataway people in early life just after colonial affairs were transferred to the Crown. By his marriage in 1708 to a member of one of the pioneer families of the Baptist Church (Mercy Drake it is supposed) the following six named children were born :

SUSANNAH, who became the wife of Joseph Hull.

BETSEY, who died young.

BENJAMIN, who married Hannah Dunn, 1739. the year his father assumed the pastorate of this church—and had four sons and four daughters. Asher, who married Mary Drake. Isaac, whose wife was Margaret Manning. Benjamin, who did not marry, Samuel, who married Elizabeth Bishop, and the daughters were Mary, who became Andrew Manning's wife ; Mercy, who married Ephraim Piatt ; Elizabeth, who married Joseph Stelle, and Rachel whose husbands were Ephraim F. Randolph and afterwards Samuel F. Randolph.

JOHN, the second son of Rev. Benjamin Stelle, married Rachel Thompson and was a mariner. Their children were Charity, Experience, Thompson, Lewis and Phœbe.

ISAAC was the youngest son of Rev. Benjamin Stelle, who succeeded his father in the pastorate of the church, 1759. He married Christiana Clarkson and had seven sons and two daughters, Benjamin, Ambrose, John, Abel, Joseph, Oliver, Samuel, Mary and Mercy.

RACHEL, the 'youngest child of Rev. Benjamin Stelle, married in 1734 Ephraim F. Randolph and had two sons and four daughters.

These children of Rev. Benjamin Stelle, with the offspring God gave them, have always been among the chief supporters of the Baptist Church in Piscataway and in many other communities where their lot has been cast.

To enumerate the many excellent virtues and christian graces which have characterized this family for two hundred years and more, would require another day's celebration. Such an event as the gathering of all the living who are the children and heirs of the distinguished Poncet Stelle would afford a suitable opportunity to consider the deeds of many generations, and record the wonderful experiences which link the present with the past.

CONCLUSION.

The roll call given includes the names of most of the men, who with their wives, laid the foundations of society in this locality and established its social, moral and religious character. Piscataway was from the first a plantation of christians—a colony of conscience The original settlers came here to escape religious persecution elsewhere and establish a permanent home here where they might enjoy the liberty of the gospel and the free exercise of their own spiritual convictions. May their descendants never lower the standard of religous living as set up in those pioneer days, nor manifest an indifference for such conscientious motives as actuated the early forefathers of this community.

INDEX.

www.ingramcontent.com/pod-product-compliance
Lightning Source LLC
Chambersburg PA
CBHW030622270326
41927CB00007B/1279